Language of Daniel the Prophet

LANGUAGE OF
DANIEL
THE PROPHET
Spoken Word in the First Person

JAMES C. RICHMOND

HARRIS
Author Services

WORLDWIDE

Contents

Preface

This book entitled, "The Language of Daniel" – based on the "Book of Daniel" in the Old Testament, all twelve chapters of it – is a testimony of God's revelation to me in telling the story of salvation in a poetic format. As a person whom our loving Lord gifted with the art form of poetry or spoken-word poetry, it is a sacred privilege to be inspired, to use this form of art to write and expound on these tremendous truths.

I recall coming to the end of writing the poetic verses on Daniel 12, when a giant of an angel appeared. He was imposing and awesome in power – even though I saw him only from his left side and back. Yet, his beautiful smile calmed my frightened heart. He appeared, in height, to reach into the sky – yet his appearance in its entirety was present for me to see. Afraid – yet overjoyed, anxious – yet stupified and mesmerized, I cried myself weak in praise to God. Therefore, it is with this joy in my heart that I gift this work of praise to each and every one of you.

These poetic pieces on the "Book of Daniel" arose from my need to understand biblical prophecy and to make it more palatable to a wider audience – not only the religious community. In composing these, I have drawn on my community involvement and experiences of 30 years, of hearing the discourses of many individuals about God, of questions – about whether He really exists or what or who He really is – in many debates and presentations. My words have been motivated by my studies and arduous work in Theology at Andrews University and my time at the NETS training program – along with the International Bible Institute – with some of the top theologians in the SDA Church Organization. It is my hope that these time-sensitive and urgent sermons of "the time of the end", coming from the Book of Daniel, will draw us all to the original pen of creation: Our God and soon-coming King.

It has been stated that it is not an easy feat for someone to write, complete, and publish – in poetic format or spoken-word pieces – thoughts on the entire book of Daniel. I'm humbled by this sentiment and hope that you enjoy these words – and share them in your sermons, at your morning devotions, and with all of your friends and relatives. I hope that you do so through social media platforms, too, so that men, women, and children everywhere will be drawn closer to God through the power of His word: the BIBLE.

I have certainly felt an overpowering joy at completing the writing of the excerpts in section one, together with the twelve poetic sermons, reflections, and prayers that accompany each poetic piece on each chapter of Daniel. They're intended for our communal enjoyment, enrichment, and spiritual upliftment. I mean, I'm on top of the world! Let me encourage you, now, to keep the pages turning so that you can get to the meat of the matter. Let this serve as the appetizer and the *hors d'oeuvre* before we get to the main course – then down to dessert. My prayer for us, today, is to keep "looking unto Jesus, the author and finisher of our faith, who for the joy that was set before Him endured the cross, despising the shame, and has sat down at the right hand of the throne of God (Hebrews 12:2)." Let's have a little talk, now, about the pen of creation.

Preface Continues

Pen of Creation

Who called the worlds into existence
And gloried in their coexistence
The Father, Son, and Holy Spirit in all their brilliance
Penned the worlds, then penned the clouds across the skies
Formed the stars, and sprinkled them like ink to shine 'til sunrise
Whose blessed voice called out from the blackened deep, then
divided the day from the night
The Pen of Creation, the original shining Light.

The Blessed Pen of Creation
Who vegetated the world before forming the stars, forming all from
one foundation!
The in-condescending light
Who is the embodiment of light and might!
Whilst separating the terrestrial environment
Forming all in efflorescence
Gathering the water into one

And the dry land separately; it was done
God the Father, the Holy Spirit, and the Son

Creating too, trees that bear fruits, and seed-bearing plants to serve
as food
Then nestling the Garden of Eden, where its beauty exudes

The sun and the moon, in their varying altitudes
Distilling light earthward in longitude and latitude
Placing water creatures of all kinds, birds, and land animals
This was just God's invested capital
To come to the crowning act of His creation
Of Adam the man, and Eve: the vivacious woman.

When man sinned
That's the day earth's light dimmed
And God winged upon the clouds
To clear the air of separation and man's doubts
The Pen of Creation thus pursues
Showing Adam, Eve, and everyone – His love endures,
That God is love – although His Justice must exclude
Thus, contradicting the lying serpent who feuds
When God marked His aversion to sin and shame,
The devil realized that God was up to his game
The Pen of Creation became the Pen of Salvation
And gifted His Son as a Sacrifice – for sin's eradication.

As time and events passed year by year, bringing new days,
And men continued to disobey,
God in His glorious display
Flooded the earth for forty nights and forty days
For all who sin must pay.
Triumphantly granting deliverance to Israel from Egypt, He paved
the way

A pillar of fire by night, a pillar of cloud by day
The Pen of Creation became the Pen of Salvation
In His quest to save all from damnation

For in His love and mercy
He gave a glimpse of Earth's destiny
And gave to man His Ten Commandments
Love to God and love to man – a sacred arrangement
And promised to write it in men's hearts
A Savior – the Pen of Salvation – playing His part
Whilst the Holy Spirit still convicting hearts

Using men and women to write about and tell of Jesus
Some saying: our Deliverer receive us
Never leave us nor forsake us
Whilst others will try to seize us
Still, the Pen of Creation – being the Pen of Salvation
Uses the 66 Biblical books to point out Genesis to Revelation
Using many inspired writings to show men the way to God
Whom alone must be eternally awed!
The Eternal Word: the Living Word.
Now the Pen of Creation is the Pen of Salvation

End.

Acknowledgment

– To Lady Ann, my four children: James Jr., Lisa, Levar and Ryan –

– Lu-Shawn M. Thompson, Wife of the late Brooklyn District Attorney, Ken Thompson –

– Love to God and Love to Man –

Matthew 22:35-40

Foreword

The book of Daniel has fascinated thinkers for centuries. In addition to its apocalyptic genre and language, theologians and inquiring minds have always found within its pages a wealth of theological truths that informs both our practical lives and our view of end of time. This book seeks to uniquely bring to light the message of Daniel to the contemporary mind by utilizing poetry. The author James Richmond is not endeavouring to provide a verse-by-verse commentary on the text, rather he gives the text a poetic voice articulated in everyday language. The themes of Daniel are taken from their historical context and given dynamic equivalences so that the reader is made to hear the prophetic voice in contemporary tones.

This book is based upon an historicist understanding of apocalyptic prophesy. The prophet though writing in the sixth century BC understood that most of what was written would span the whole spectrum of history culminating with the Second Advent. In reading the book of Daniel the reader is not left to imagine the season or the reason for the unfolding of end time events, events are shown to be set within a chronological spectrum. History is seen not at the mere recollection of facts that is arbitrarily strewn over time, rather, it is purposive and providentially orchestrated. The divine factor in history stands clear upon the pages of Daniel. The reader is not merely amused by information but there is personal appeal that is made to encounter in a personal way the God of prophecy.

The second section of this book captures the ethos of each chapter of Daniel through the art of poetry. The reflections and prayers that follows allow the reader to practical synthesise and imbibe the main message of each passage. The ardent student of scripture would find interesting insights for theological reflection therein. The literary mind would also find in these poems a vast reservoir of gems to titillate the imagination and ruminate upon. The author has skilfully decoded without the apocalyptic overtures of Daniel into a language that is both relatable and congenial to the modern ear.

In a world where many are seeking answers beyond the trivialities of life, and where the mind is inundated with speculative theories about the future and the end of the age, the book of Daniel offers higher perspectives on these issues. The answers to this mundane reality have been etched in the holy writ. God is posited as having the final word on the course of history, He guides the affairs of this world, leaders in every sphere are His instruments, kingdoms are determined at His behest, and time will end when He deems it is right. The God of heaven is not as some paint Him to be—removed and disinterested in the daily affairs of his creation, to the contrary He is intimately involved and acutely aware of everything.

This volume will prove to be a blessing to the inquiring mind, as well as those whose knowledge of Daniel is still in its elementary stages; both are plunged into the riches of apocalyptic thinking made simple yet profound. The goal at the end of this journey still remains the same as was with the author of Daniel—to show the sovereignty of

God over His creation. This book was written with a salvific purpose as its goal, I pray that you may discover that purpose as you read. -Mario Phillip, PhD.

Introduction

What is the purpose of this book?

It is to give meaning to this life that we are privileged to live, knowing that God is ever-present to save. To be upfront and totally clear, this book is not a commentary on the Book of Daniel but, rather, an expression of my understanding of my personal relationship with God and a demonstration of the text in a special poetic format. This is an exposition of God using every means to touch the heart of mankind. On this journey, we will see what God originally intended for Man at creation and what God has in store for man as a new creation. The Book of Daniel was written in two languages. The beginning of it was written in Hebrew, right up to chapter 2 verse 3, and in Aramaic from chapter 2 verse 4 to the ending of chapter 7 – which correlates with the domination of the Jews. However, in chapter 8, onwards to the end, the Book returns to its original written Hebrew writing. The naming of my book, "The Language of Daniel", comes out of this reality. I have chosen the Book of Daniel – a book of poetic expressions in its own right – and, using the talent in poetry entrusted to me, dramatize God's guidance, forgiveness, and grace in our lives. It is another way to proclaim my confidence in my belief in an awesome, forgiving, loving, delivering, and lifesaving God. My poetic expressions are born out of my quest to figure out the prophetic meanings in a way that piques interest in the word of the Living God. I hope to show where we are and how we have arrived at this point in time in the Earth's history; worshipping different gods, having differing opinions, and believing – or having no belief whatsoever – in the prospect of there being anything greater than ourselves. Did all of these things actually happen as represented in the Bible? Did all these things happen in the Book of Daniel? Could this all be just a big fat lie, perpetuated by mankind? Maybe, just maybe, men and women had been inspired by the Almighty God to record these factual stories of salvation to drive our faith. Could the teachings of the Bible be proven correct? Is its influence as great today as it was in the days of Daniel?

Looking back on the experiences of my life, I can declare that there is a God that has saved me time and again from many situations. I was in one particular situation that left me badly wounded and utterly disfigured in my younger days; I can testify to His saving grace. He has also helped me at other times relating to sickness or death, and with situations that could have found me mentally deprived of my faculties or expired in the body: dead. Therefore, it is my belief and my hope in God that has enabled me to stand despite all fears – not because I'm fearless! I stand in confidence on the solid rock of Christ (Psalm 18:2) for all other ground is sinking sand! (Matthew 7:24-27). What a great joy it is to have a relationship with God!

It is my hope that you can taste and see that the Lord is good (Psalm 34:8). I challenge you, today, to stop denying yourself the privilege of entering into a saving relationship with your Creator. Denying yourself this joy can be likened to ingesting poison – the poisonous

2

parts of life – and just waiting to embrace eternal damnation. The only antidote for the neglect is just a little step to start building this precious relationship. Daniel had a relationship with God and, as a result, was given the interpretation of Nebuchadnezzar's dream. I encourage you to read Daniel, chapter 2; you will learn the story of the Earth's destiny. Just know that God's promises are always upheld; He will never leave you nor forsake you (Psalm 25:14, Amos 3:7, John 15:14-15, Deuteronomy 31:6).

It is time to stop doubting, or procrastinating – just taste and see that the Lord is good. As a people, of God, we hope for something better (Psalm 34:8). This hope – which burns from within – transcends even the grave. It is this hope that keeps us going and for which we strive – for the prize of the high calling of Christ. If we can only connect our experiences in life to a realization that there is a God who loves us so maddeningly, we would know that, as well as Jesus who died in our stead, His angels are also pitched in battles against the fallen angels in protecting us, every minute of the day. We who worship God can attest to trials faced and victories gained. However, we long for the soon return of the Savior, Jesus Christ. Let it be known and let it be proclaimed that it is God's love for us that caused Him to give His only begotten Son – an active member of the Godhead – to die to redeem us after Man's sin separated us from Him. The Bible paints a truly fascinating account and testimony of God's deliverance and love for His creation.

In this book, readers will experience the beauty of the biblical text of Daniel in two ways. Firstly, readers will be presented with an excerpt of each chapter. Secondly, they will get the opportunity to digest my poetic response to the biblical text in each chapter. Also, I will help in opening their eyes to see the beauty and structure of the book of

Daniel from my own poetic utterances, which will hopefully lead the reader to the worship of God, bringing them to a state of worship and awe of the Creator of the universe.

Prayer – My God and soon-coming King! I'm not what I would like to be; make me a better recipient of your love. Please give me your protection; let it rain from your throne of grace above. Make me worthy of your marvelous grace! I'm not asking to be the richest, nor asking for titles, nor asking for positions – but ask that you please help me each and every day to be a better witness in the way that I live and interact with everyone. I know my limitations; keep my focus on you for I'm still sinful, despite giving my heart to you. Please forgive me and wash my sins away. Gift to me the knowledge in understanding your word, and to share to all, the power of your love. I pray in the name of our Loving Lord and Savior. Jesus Christ, Amen.

SECTION I

–

Age of COVID-19

In the age of COVID-19
Millions infected: deaths routine
Hundreds of thousands of deaths: living life in a sordid dream
Light of compassion disappears; how can you glorify God? glorify God
The light, Fire, and Seed: Bread of the Living Word!

Know that God truly cares: The Lord is terrific
In light and reality of the pandemic
Fire of conviction in limited epistemic
Life so sacred; to breathe so traumatic
Seed of negligence, the rising sadness of death, and sentences, sentences
The Bread of the Word: with no pretenses!

For in darkness of COVID-19 and its strains, hearts are crushed with fear
Reaching for the great plan of salvation: heart of gold loving and dear
It is written: the word is the fullest revelation of Jesus – of Jesus, of Jesus

It is us who crucify us
It is us who crucify us!

"Life is not a perfect script, but you can rewrite the scenes
Let the substance of hope and belief, grow into actionable themes
The necessary ingredient, which is faith, propels into fulfilling
dreams"

What Makes Daniel So Unique

It is the story of a young man's discernment, commitment, and fulfillment of God in his life. His dedication to God, finds him triumphant in the face of his journey and years of exile in Babylon, with several other young nobles of the day, triumphant unto the time of the end of his life and days. It tells of Daniel's unfailing loyalty and steadfast dependence on God. He was loyal to God and similarly loyal to his duties of state in both Babylon and Medo-Persia. He was a friend of God and a friend to man. Herein, we find that the prophet Daniel placed complete emphasis on the total and absolute sovereignty of God – in both the historical and prophetic sections of the book. When all seems lost and daunting, Daniel points us to the supreme Creator of Heaven and Earth through his reliance and utter confidence in God (Daniel 4:17).

The book of Daniel gives an amazing timeline of the coming of the Messiah: the ultimate Savior (Daniel 9:24-27). Also, there are many practical lessons one can learn for living from Daniel, chapter 1 to chapter 6. First and foremost, one must be determined to be faithful to God. This is the first duty of mankind: to serve God with all of your heart and all of your soul (Deuteronomy 22:5). We should come boldly to His throne of grace, knowing that He will keep His end of the bargain, showing mercy (Hebrews 4:6). Our God is faithful and true, and He expects us to, likewise, be faithful to Him. The book of Daniel itself begins with the historical and, having progressed into chapter 7, presents the vision of the future of the Jewish people.

In Daniel 8 and 9, we consider the political entities of history – with Babylon omitted this time – through medieval Christianity, and signposted more directly to Christ's work of atonement and salvation from sin. This makes it possible for sinners to become saints so that they can inherit the Kingdom of God.

Daniel 10 to Daniel 12 dramatize the battle and the sure deliverance of the people of God. The invisible powers and spiritual influences on nations in the world are laid bare for all to see. It is heartening to know, though, that God's spiritual beings are constantly on the march, carrying out His purpose in this world of sin to defend and protect His people (Exodus 12:23; 2 Samuel 24:16).

I Know I Am a Christian

When all the pain and the hurt of life beset my day
And the tears of despair cloud my way
When all the unending trials and tribulations keep bashing me, day
after day
Though God seems far away
When the doubt – the doubt with little hope – causes me to pray

Then I know I am a Christian

When all around me, 'tis like sinking sand
And the difficulties are more than I can understand
When everything I do seems in vain
Education, fame, and the ignoble gain
The hurt and the pain – the hurt and the pain keep recurring again

Still, I am a Christian

When my shout is like a silent cry
And my heart sinks within and dies
When my mouth dares not testify
And all my faults are justified
Dear Lord, I pray! Save me

Still, I say I am a Christian

When God is my only hope
And the only way that I can cope
Though my faith is strong yet still there's lingering doubt
Then my silent cry is like a loud shout
Lord! I pray thee: my soul to keep

I am a Christian

When the darkness seems to separate my God from me
And the darkness of sin condemns me and clouds my destiny
Lord! Let me hold on, for faith is the victory

Let me cling still to the cross of Calvary
O Lord, I pray! Save me

I know I am a Christian

End.

Ask the Savior

Ask the Savior to give to you strength
When all seems lost, in distress, and lament:
How can you not know what His sacrifice meant?
How can you not know that His blood which flowed
On Calvary Hill – where His salvific power endured
With the essence of Omnipotent love bestowed –
Truly is the beginning and ending of love untold?

Ask the Savior to forgive and show you His love
For the poor in spirit will inherit the Kingdom of God above
How can you not know that He can wash away the painful flood?
How can you not know that, though living in sin,
It only takes a prayer? It only takes a prayer to win
With favor and forgiveness – which comes from Him,
Flowing like a fountain, from the throne of Christ the King.

Ask the Savior, the blessed Son of God,
Why the laws embody the love of God
How can you not know that He is Lord?
How can you not know that God the Father, God the Son, and God
the Holy Spirit
Created the heavens and earth, and formed man from the very dust

of it
Then kissed the breath of life in gentle love with His Holy Spirit
And wrapped His loving embrace, as a protective shield, across the
summit.

End.

Daniel One Excerpt

There are many practical lessons one can learn for living from Daniel chapter one to chapter six. First and foremost, one must be determined to be faithful to God. This is the first duty of mankind: to serve God with all of your heart and all of your soul (Deuteronomy 22:5). We should come boldly to His throne of grace, knowing that He will keep His end of the bargain, showing mercy (Hebrews 4:6). Our God is faithful and true – and He expects us to, likewise, be faithful to Him.

It must be stated that Daniel the prophet was born into an upper-class Jewish family from Palestine around 622 BC. He spent his childhood in Judea – or in the Kingdom of Judah – and his adulthood in the Kingdom of Babylon, for he was taken into captivity in the first invasion of Nebuchadnezzar in the summer of 605 BC. The prophet Daniel was approximately 17 years old at the time. Whilst in captivity, Daniel, Hananiah, Mishael, and Azariah were expected to eat the King's meat and drink the King's wine, yet they decided not to do so; they desired to honor God by not eating unclean meat or meat offered to idols, and not to partake in his wine because of their belief and worship of the Creator God (Exodus 34:15, Proverbs 20:1).

However, they found a way in which they were able to obey their God while not bringing displeasure and problems to the eunuch.

It is our duty as Christians to be wise as a serpent so that no harm will come to others in our decision-making, regardless of the situation we face (Matthew 10:16). We need to say, like Daniel to our Melzar, (Daniel 1:12) "Prove thy servants, I beseech thee, ten days; and let them give us pulse to eat, and water to drink", whilst being faithful to our Loving Lord, in every testing situation. You must not forget the spiritual diet (the word of God – Psalm 119:105) that brought you this far, nor the prescribed diet (acceptable food – Genesis 1:29) to sustain you physically, that God requires of a faithful steward. We should never forget the spiritual diet, nor the diet we are accustomed to, for any other diet that clouds the mind can serve to separate us from God. The Bible states that "wine is a mocker, strong drink is raging: and whosoever is deceived thereby is not wise" (Proverbs 20:1), and has the power to further demoralize someone ("Give strong drink unto him that is ready to perish, and wine unto those that be of heavy hearts" (Proverbs 31:6). Despite being in captivity, just remember that there is an appointed time for liberty and, therefore, remain focused on living your faith. Remember that God is always in the business of deliverance, but in the deliverance of a faithful people. Daniel eventually lived a fascinating life. God inspired his writing of the Book of Daniel to give us an understanding of the time of the end and to draw us all to Him.

The dating and authorship of the Book of Daniel should be of utmost importance to all students of the Bible because this is very instructive. It is traditionally believed that Daniel wrote the Book in the sixth century BC according to the Book of Daniel (7:1-2, 15; 8:1; 9:1; 10:2; 12:4-5), as Jesus Himself mentioned in the Book of

Matthew 24:15 ("Wherefore ye therefore shall see [the] abomination of desolation, spoken of by Daniel the prophet, stand in the holy place..."), and the witness account of Josephus: a Jewish historian who died around AD 100. Given the historical facts that are in the Book of Daniel, we can only conclude that it was written in the sixth century BC because only someone living in that time would have had knowledge of these facts. We know that these facts were lost after the sixth century and only recovered in recent times by means of archaeological discoveries. Even the Babylonian cuneiform tablets which mention Belshazzar confirm the authorship of the Book of Daniel. The manuscript discoveries at Qumran also show the popularity of the Book of Daniel and show how it was revered and cited as scripture in the second century BC by the Jewish sect, known as the Essenes. Also, there cannot be a more credible account of a true witness to the authorship of the Book of Daniel than the book itself, the historian Josephus, and certainly the savior Jesus Christ Himself.

However, historical-critical scholars believe that it was written in the Maccabean period of the second century BC. The Maccabean era is named after the Maccabee family, who led the revolt in 167 BC against the Syrian King Antiochus IV Epiphanes – who reigned from 175–163 BC, including over Judah. It is important to note that they established an independent Jewish state from 142 BC to 63 BC until the Roman general Pompey conquered Jerusalem and Judah became a Roman province. The Maccabean thesis claims that the second-century date and authorship of Daniel is rooted in the work of an unknown writer who either wrote or edited the Book at that time and that the prophecies were written after the event. It was written to provide meaning and encouragement in the context of the mid-second century Jewish religious struggle; the time periods refer to literal days, not years.

The Seventh-day Adventist view follows the historical method of prophetic interpretation in explaining the symbols and their meanings. It is also referred to as the "historicist method" or the "continuous historical method". It accepts the fact that the prophecies of Daniel and Revelation are intended to find fulfillment in historical time – in the final establishment of God's eternal Kingdom. The Adventist believes in the year-day principle of a symbolic day which equals a literal year. This year-day method is integral to the Adventist view so that we can anticipate the schedule of the predicted events. Even Jesus used the historicist method in interpreting Daniel in declaring, "The time is fulfilled, and the Kingdom of God is at hand" (Mark 1:15). Jesus, even in affirming the prophetic fulfillment, alluded to Daniel's 70-week prophecy of Daniel 9:24-27 that foretold the appearance of the Messiah. Ellen G. White states that "When the books of Daniel and Revelation are better understood, believers will have an entirely different religious experience. They will be given such glimpses of the open gates of heaven that heart and mind will be impressed with the character that all must develop in order to realize the blessedness which is to be the reward of the pure in heart" (*Testimonies to Ministers*, p. 114). Obviously, White subscribed to the historicist method of prophetic interpretation. I must declare that the Adventist view makes the most sense to me, especially because of the year-day method.

Daniel Two Excerpt

Throughout history and time immemorial, God has remained constant and central in the affairs of Man. In every situation, in every event, God has always reserved for Himself individuals who will stand for what is right and pleasing in His sight, regardless of adverse circumstances. In this chapter, the emphasis is placed on prayer, as Daniel prayed constantly by himself. However, as the death decree was given, Daniel sought out his friends for corporate prayer. Many of us do not even have a prayer life. We seldom give ourselves to prayer. Even in the churches today, some members do not have a prayer life. Many of our church doors are closed on Sunday evening. During the week, and at Wednesday night prayer meetings, only a very few members would show up for mid-week service. However, when faced with difficult and heartrending situations, those are the times we will run into our closets or run to the church, asking for prayers for ourselves and our family. We know prayer works! It is Jesus who said, "Again I say unto you, that if two of you shall agree on earth as touching anything that they shall ask, it shall be done for them of my Father which is in heaven. For where two or three are gathered together in my name, there am I in the midst of them" (Matthew 18:19-20). Therefore, our prayer life is very important for victorious living.

It is not fortuitous that God set aside Daniel and his three Hebrew relatives to remind the people of Judah, that if you stand with Him, He'll stand with you. Our God is saying to you today that you should remember Him, despite being in bondage. In every aspect of life, you should pay homage. Despite the trials and tribulations that come your way on a daily basis, despite friends and relatives who might put stumbling blocks in your way – and health situations that threaten your life and existence – remember God will never leave you nor forsake you. To avail yourself of God's power, we are called to be special: "But ye are a chosen generation, a royal priesthood, a holy nation, a peculiar people; that ye should shew forth the praises of him who hath called you out of darkness into his marvelous light: 1 Peter 2:9".

The prophet Daniel came from an upper-class Jewish family, with access to the best education of the day. His parents trained him from a child to develop a habit of strict temperance. He was taught to conform to nature's laws, and his eating and drinking had a direct influence upon his physical, mental, and moral nature. It is even proffered by the Jewish historian Josephus that Daniel, Shadrach, Meshach, and Abednego were related to King Zedekiah. Given the constant fear of invasion and captivity that must have permeated Judah at that time, they were obviously prepared by their parents and teachers to honor and stand for God in any given situation. The threat of captivity was real; for some families, it was important to instill knowledge of God in their children. Imagine thinking that, if taken into captivity, your choice is to worship idols or suffer severely. Imagine growing up knowing the God of Heaven but now having to stand in line to worship inanimate objects. Therefore, it's obvious that these young men, having been taught well, purposed in their hearts to follow the teaching – and belief in the true and living God and triumphed (Daniel 1:8-16).

It is pellucidly clear to me that their hearts' songs were to be faithful so that they would honor their parents, and honor God, at every time, at every place, in every way. They knew not to eat food offered to idols; they knew not to eat unclean foods. They knew that they served a God who could rain down bread from heaven as He did for their ancestors in the wilderness (Exodus 16:4). They knew that this same God could deliver and keep them in His care. I, therefore, submit to you that they were prepared – aware of the times, and events, they were living in – so their attitudes were resolute and uncompromising.

Are we to stand resolute as well as Daniel and the three Hebrew boys? We cannot do otherwise in these trying times of the end.

It is quite clear that Daniel chapter two gives an individual a better grasp of how to grapple with both the Book of Daniel and the Book of Revelation. The chapter emphatically states that God reveals deep and mysterious things (Daniel 2:22, 2:47). In reading the expositions of C. Mervyn Maxwell in *God Cares*, volume one, one can gain remarkable clarity from the gleaming jewels of knowledge that lie within the pages of the Book of Daniel. His explanation of Daniel two is spot on in that the central theme is, indeed, that God knows about the future and reveals the part that is for us to know.

However, Doukhan's emphasis is on the role Daniel plays as a prophet of reference for early Christian tradition. Apart from Christian philosophers who were attracted to the Book, Islam remembers Daniel as one who predicts the future. I am fascinated by Doukhan's theory of the "feet of iron and clay" of the image. He

21

states that some have said that Jesus set up His Kingdom when He was on earth approximately 2,000 years ago. However, this cannot be so because the supernatural stone didn't hit the head of the image (Babylon), or the chest of silver (Medo-Persia), or the brass of the belly and thighs (Greece), nor the legs of iron (Rome), but the feet and toes of clay and iron; "in the days of those kings", the stone would hit the image on its feet of iron and clay. At that time, God would set up a Kingdom that would never be destroyed (Daniel 2:44).

The Babylon Empire was established in 605 BC – when Nebuchadnezzar ruled as king – and came to its end in 539 BC. It was known as the "Head of Gold" due to the fact that it was the most glorious kingdom (Daniel 2:38-40). The Medo-Persia Empire lasted from 539 BC to 331 BC, known as the "Breast and Arms of Silver". This Kingdom had two parts and matches the part of the image with the two arms (Daniel 2:32), and Alexander the Great, founder of the Greek Empire, in 331 BC vanquished the Medes and Persians to establish the Greek Empire, which managed to survive on to 168 BC – Belly and Thighs of Brass, due to its soldiers who wore armor made of Bronze (Daniel 2:32). In 168 BC Rome became the dominant power in the Mediterranean, bringing in the fourth Empire of the statue prophecy until 476 AD – Iron Kingdom, (Daniel 2:40).

Daniel Three Excerpt

In this chapter, we find Shadrach, Meshach, and Abednego in deep trouble, because they did not bow down and worship the golden image (Daniel 2:5-6). In life we are faced with our golden image when others want us to bow down, compromising our Christian principles. Also, our young people are under constant attack by the enemy, with peer pressure; to do as the Romans do, compromising their belief and thereby being drawn away from the church. Many of our young people who were born into the church are today living in the world, bowing down to varying images of life that are taking them to the ways of losing their soul's salvation. Some are even giving up honoring the seventh-day sabbath of their God and savior. We need to realize that any situation that would draw us away from giving God glory, is a situation that we should stand firmly against. It is important for all to be reminded that just as how Babylon of King Nebuchadnezzar demanded worship, spiritual Babylon would also require worship of the image to the beast (Revelation 13). We should stand like the brave or stand like the three Hebrew boys and we will see our salvation come about in every instance (Daniel 3:24-26).

It is reported though that in 2015, of all firefighters who died, 35% of them died fighting fires. I can only imagine how their families feel when these brave men are called out to confront fires as they carry out their daily duties. I can only imagine the unbearable heat they face, the loss of life in their experience, of both occupants of the properties and even firefighters, due to the immense heat and blazing fires. Therefore, I can only imagine the heat that emanated from the specially constructed fiery furnace of Babylon. It was intended for execution and obviously specially constructed to detract opponents of the king from going up against him. Many obviously lost their lives in that fiery furnace before. However, on the day that the three Hebrew boys were cast into that furnace, it was seven times hotter. The strong men of Babylon, who threw the three Hebrew boys in, died on the very spot because of the intense heat. Fortunately, though, the three Hebrew boys had a Savior, a deliverer!

Daniel Four Excerpt

In chapter four of Daniel, King Nebuchadnezzar again had a dream. However, it came this time as a tree in the midst of the earth (Daniel 4:10), and this tree grew strong and reached heaven (v11). In giving the interpretation of this dream, Daniel was very careful at first. Nevertheless, he ended up giving the full meaning of the entire dream. In life when many of us achieve riches and prestige, we oftentimes become pompous and full of pride. We forget God, we forget the poor, we forget to give the glory to God, and not to ourselves. This is where our downfall usually comes. Sometimes the stump is left for us to go back to when we have seen our bad ways and repent, or sometimes many died and leave the riches behind because they cannot change and humble themselves to the God who allowed them to attain the riches or the position of power. Our testimony must always be in praise to God for His wonderful kindness towards us, for health, for strength, and for sustenance. When Nebuchadnezzar lifted up his eyes to acknowledge the God of Heaven, everything was restored. It is important for everyone to realize that God does not like anyone, poor or powerful, to give the praise that is due to Him to themselves or to other gods. This chapter is the testimony of a redeemed king to all people, nations, and languages, that dwell in all the earth (v1), giving honor and glory to the real King of kings (Daniel 4:37). The leaders of the world today should take a page out of the redeemed life of king Nebuchadnezzar.

Daniel Five Excerpt

King Belshazzar giving a great feast to a thousand of his leading cabinet members and his leaders of the day and their wives, or to be more biblically correct, his lords and their wives. He was having a great time and decided to use the sacred vessels that were taken out from the temple of the house of God which was at Jerusalem (Daniel 5:3). Although, Belshazzar knew about his grandfather Nebuchadnezzar's pompousness and what he experienced; in his drunken state he decided to test the patience of God by drinking wine in them and praising gods of gold, of silver, of brass, of iron, of wood, and of stone. I wonder why many of us feel that we can do what is pleasing in our sight, praising ourselves, looking to inanimate objects to give praise, and God who gave us the breath of life in the first place should just accept. We were created to give God all the praise and all the glory (Psalm 115:1, 96:4-9).

It is important to interject that Daniel lived an exemplary life and left the example that when Man is paired in communion with God, allowing God to lead, though kingdoms of evil will rise, and kingdoms will fall; God's love, esteem, and deliverance remains steadfast and sure to the faithful (Daniel 10:11). Despite the conniving ways and traps of man, God delivers every-time even from the lion's den or from the fiery furnace, where Shadrack, Meshack, and Abednego were thrown (Daniel 3:23-25). Daniel's faithfulness to God allowed him to be appointed time and again into the leadership of successive kingdoms and governments. He was appointed in charge of the government of Babylon and the government of Medo-Persia – although he was not without his detractors and antagonists (Daniel 6:15-16).

We should be reminded that Daniel's God, is the same God yesterday, today, and forever. We serve an awesome God. He is the great King of kings and Lord of lords, the author and finisher of our faith (Hebrews 12:2), who sits high and looks low (Psalm 138:6), but decided to use inanimate metal of gold, silver, bronze, iron, and the substance of clay to tell the historical destiny of the world. Where each of those inanimate metal shows the deteriorating and decreasing value and strength of the quality of the four world powers (Daniel 2) and of our troublous times.

When your back is against the wall, He delivers! When all seems lost, He delivers! When you're in your fiery furnace experience, He delivers! He is a God who delivers on time. His love permeates the Bible, pointing us to the New Jerusalem. We first read of Jerusalem and Babylon in the Book of Genesis and, lastly, in the Book of Revelation. However, midway in between the books of Genesis and Revelation, we find the anointed verse of Daniel 9:26, describing the crucifixion of the Savior. Then, later on in Daniel 12:1, we catch a glimpse of the alleluia verse and glorious time when Christ Jesus descends to deliver his children. You stand for Him; He stands for you and delivers!

Daniel Six Excerpt

In chapter six we have a unique situation of jealousy. The main theme is worship, worship to the king, or worship to the true God. Darius the king was obviously placing the most competent individuals into a leadership position but elevated Daniel over the others (Daniel 6:2-3) and they were not pleased. To begin, he was a Jew and they had more rights to the leadership of the kingdom. They were incensed and decided to conspire against Daniel. They could not find any fault against Daniel, so they deceived the king into passing a decree to worship him for one month. If anyone petitioned or prayed to any other man or god within that thirty days, they should be cast into the lion's den. This is one of the most popular, dramatic, inspirational stories in all of scripture about how God delivers those who worship Him, regardless of the circumstances (Psalm 107:6, 2 Corinthians 10:3-4)

In considering the historical and archaeological context of Daniel, with our lens focusing on chapter one to chapter six, we'll find an amazing array of information that only serves to strengthen our faith in a soon-coming Savior (Daniel 2:44-45, 7:14). In the greater scheme of things historically, we must be thankful for the way God has demonstrated His love towards us throughout time, from creation down to the days of Daniel and beyond.

In 605 BC, history took another turn when King Nebuchadnezzar of Babylon conquered the Kingdom of Judah and the capital city, Jerusalem (Daniel 1:2). In the midst of those captives that he took were four young men, including Daniel. They bore witness to the awesome power of the God of Heaven and His demonstrable love and saving grace throughout their captivity and lifetimes. Whilst Daniel six is the last historical chapter, the Book of Daniel confirms that God used a king, a prophet, and a significant dream of a king to tell about the time of the end, and of two cities – Babylon and Jerusalem – two systems – righteousness and evil (Amos 14-15) – and the future of man (Romans 15:13). We can reconstruct and confirm history through known facts of the past and, certainly, through archeology. However, we can find knowledge within the pages of the Bible, from Genesis to Revelation, and most certainly within the Book of Daniel for our benefit to educate us about the past, the future, and the promised salvation of Jesus. This will enable us to give Him all the praise and worship He deserves. We will all face our lion's den.

Imagine with me the terrible disappointment and pain of a woman upon returning home, only to receive a severe physical trashing from her husband because she was out "too long" and "too late" whilst accusing her of cheating. Imagine the terrible fear she feels, the terrible psychological shock, and the terrible loss of trust in their relationship. How abusive can a husband be? How unfair can some men be toward their spouse, without investigating the facts of the situation, much more meting out physical judgment indiscriminately? What about the damage done to the children as a result of the abuse? What about the effects on her relatives, friends, and neighbors? Also, imagine a man being accosted by his wife and given the same treatment.

Now, imagine with me another woman, returning home, and being greeted by her husband with loving concern about her wellbeing, her exhaustion, and whether she is all right and well.

Similarly, a man being greeted in all love by his beautiful bride. The demonstration of genuine concern for another is so much better. We are rather fortunate that we serve a caring, loving God who is a fair judge. He investigates first, then passes judgment after (John 7:51). The most awesome thing about our Loving Lord is that He provides a way for sinners. He provides an advocate (1 John 2:1). It is important to state that judging or passing judgment is a very serious affair. Ask many of the judges in our courts about their experiences and awesome responsibility.

In light of God's love, we can say that God is an energetic lover. He loves His creation! Astronomers believe that God created billions of galaxies, yet He cares for the redemption of His earthly children (Ephesians 1:7). The creative love of God is self-evident and He shows up on time; He comes "on a cherub, and flew: He came swiftly upon the wings of the wind (Psalm 18:10).

Daniel Seven Excerpt

The pre-advent judgment hinges on this very text and cannot be more emphasized in this time of the end because it is scripturally based (Daniel 7:9-14). This is the foundation of investigative judgment. It is the reason we proclaim Jesus as Lord of lords and King of kings – because we are redeemed by the blood of the Lamb. All must be judged, both righteous and the wicked (Ecclesiastes 12:14). The judgment begins at the house of God (1 Peter 4:17). We are given a unique and clear understanding of the Book of Daniel from the knowledge that all must be judged (Revelation 14:6-7; 20:12).

The Book of Daniel is more than occupied with the future (Daniel 2:19, 27-28). It seems like it's bursting at its seams to give the prophetic message and interpretations; Daniel chapter seven does not disappoint. We have discovered that Daniel chapter two gives a general panoramic view of the future from King Nebuchadnezzar's time, down to the second coming of the Savior. However, this dream of Daniel extends the time period between the end of the Roman Empire and the second coming in a most dramatic fashion. In Daniel chapter two, the empire is depicted from a political standpoint; the emphasis is placed on Nebuchadnezzar's rulership and Daniel and his three Hebrew friends rise to political prominence (Daniel 2:48-49).

In Daniel chapter seven, it includes and exudes the spiritual powers that permeate the world (Daniel 8:14). Even scholars and interpreters have acknowledged the parallelism of Daniel two and Daniel seven. It is clearly emphasized in Daniel chapter seven between the fourth empire and the second coming of the symbolic falling stone which becomes a great mountain that ends up filling the earth. This is the period when the religiopolitical power will grow and persecute the followers of God.

The views presented are quite informative, clear, impressive, and factual. It is a treasure trove of knowledge for any student of Daniel, the Bible, and of history. It brings clarity to our times and certainly to the prophecy of Daniel seven which speaks about our time of the end and parallels the vision of the image of King Nebuchadnezzar in chapter two. We have discovered that it is the last chapter, written in Aramaic, that links to the preceding chapters. However, this vision of the four beasts – as seen by Daniel – connects unmistakably with the later chapters. written in Hebrew – whilst Daniel two gives a general panoramic view of the future from Nebuchadnezzar's day up to the second coming, detailing the empires from a political and military aspect. Daniel seven, though, enlarges on the time period between the fourth empire of Rome to the second coming. This makes Daniel seven a significant chapter, indicating that – between the fourth empire and the Second Advent, symbolized by the stone cut out of the mountain without hands (Daniel 2:34) – a religiopolitical power, which grows from a small beginning to world domination, will persecute the people of God.

We discover, here, that the fourth beast and the horns are not presented independently of each other in the prophecy but, rather, as a continuation of its activities. These horns correspond with the iron and clay of the feet and toes of the image not mingling. It represents the European nations that emerged from the Roman Empire. Historical records show that the European nations evolved from the Germanic tribes which destroyed the Roman Empire, for they emerged out of the demise of political Rome.

When God judges, he is fair and just. Everything is open and not hidden. In the judgment scene, we observe that "the thrones were cast down, and the Ancient of days did sit…." (Daniel 7:9). God is portrayed as traveling from some other part of Heaven in order to commence the work of the investigative judgment. Immediately after the Ancient of Days was seated, the judgment began: "in the night visions", there came "with the clouds of Heaven" "one like the Son of Man"; He "came to the Ancient of Days and was presented before Him" (Daniel 7:13). This is the judgment we should all emulate in our relationships: an orderly and just judgment. The place is overwhelming in splendor and grandeur, with the Ancient of Days, as the supreme Judge, seated on His throne, surrounded by thousands upon thousands of angels. This is an open and fair investigating process. This is not the final judgment of Revelation 20, but the investigative judgment prior to the Second Coming of Jesus.

The Book of Revelation 20:12-15 speaks about "books that are opened" and out of which the dead will be judged on the basis of "what they had done". The Book of Revelation states that "another book was opened, which is the book of life". Also, Malachi 3:16 refers to "a book of remembrance" which is written about "those who feared the Lord and thought on His name". In the Old Testament, we find that many of the prophets, including Isaiah, Jeremiah, and Micah, frequently use language and imagery that portrays God's judgment. The nations and Israel are arrayed before God, and the facts are stated, inquiries are made, and reasoning is solicited (Isaiah 1; 43:8-13, 22-28). Also, the nations "are to present their arguments and state their case in [the] public examination of the issues involved". The implications are clear in Isaiah 43:26:"Put me in remembrance; let us plead together, declare thou, that thou mayest be justified".

According to 2 Peter 2:6, Jude 1:7, Deuteronomy 29:3, and Isaiah 1:10, the divine judgment upon Sodom and Gomorrah was an "example," or a pattern. The fact that the New Testament represents the Sodom and Gomorrah judgment of eternal fire as a "pattern" judgment encourages us to view God's handling of the whole event. It is well to remember that the biblical retelling is dominated by Yahweh's prior investigation with its "justice" dialogue (Genesis 18:19), (Eric C. Livingston). The way God depicts this pattern judgment is quite significant, and the Book of Genesis 18 and 19 describes God's deliberations prior to His punitive judgment. It is clear that the "investigative judgment" concept has a variety of presentations. Certainly, it means that the righteous – as well as the wicked – will be judged. It is heartwarming to study and to understand, the great language of the Book of Daniel.

Daniel Eight Excerpt

Beginning in Daniel 8, we go through the political entities of history, omitting Babylon this time, through medieval Christianity, and point more directly to Christ's work of atonement and salvation from sin, which makes it possible for sinners to become saints, so that they can inherit the Kingdom of God. In verse 13, we hear the discourse of the two saints and the first asking, "how long shall be the vision concerning the daily sacrifices, and the transgression of desolation." The answer is given in verse 14, "unto two thousand and three hundred days; then shall the sanctuary be cleansed." We are given front row seats in the explanation of the major players in Daniel 8. It speaks about a ram, a goat, and a little horn. The Angel Gabriel informs us that the ram represents Medo-Persia and the goat represents Greece. Also, the great horn that is between the eyes of the goat is the first king of Greece. This represents the third world kingdom, which is Greece, and the great horn represents Alexander the Great. The four horns are Alexander's generals, Cassander, Ptolemy, Antigonus, and Seleucus; who succeeded him after his death in 323 BC.

Some alluded that the little horn represents Antiochus Epiphanes: the

Seleucid king who ruled over Palestine in the second century B.C (although it is clear that the little horn represents Rome).

Therefore, we must not be misled or fooled in our understanding of the 2300 days prophecy. The prevailing views of the majority of most Christians are that this prophecy relates to a literal 2300 days and will be at the time of the end. However, the main concern or cry, here, is about the desolation of the sanctuary and when it will be restored. According to Daniel 8:14, "Unto two thousand and three hundred days; then shall the sanctuary be cleansed." The saints are crying for justice and hoping for the judgment of mankind to commence. Therefore, it is very important to note the beginning and end of this 2300 days prophecy. According to (Ezra 7:25, 26), Artaxerxes gave a decree to Ezra to rebuild Jerusalem. It was a decree given in the seventh year of Artaxerxes, which gave Jerusalem its legal birth. This view makes the most sense in the interpretation of Daniel eight.

Everyone should be made aware of the truth concerning the desolation of the sanctuary for the period of the 2300 days prophecy. We are told about the pre-advent judgment that is held by seventh-day Adventists at the end of the 2300 days prophesy and the beginning of the cleansing of the heavenly sanctuary. It cannot be more strongly emphasized, and it must be proclaimed around the world today – more than ever before. It is rooted in the scriptural text of Daniel (7:9-14). This is the foundation of investigative judgment. It is the reason that, as Christians, we proclaim Jesus as Lord of Lords and King of Kings – because we are redeemed by His blood.

We must maintain a correct understanding of Daniel 8:9-14 – because it is important for all Bible-believing Christians, knowing that this message is an important pillar of the sanctuary doctrine.

Today, most Christians still believe that Daniel eight was fulfilled in the days of the Syrian king Antiochus IV Epiphanes, whom they identify with the little horn. Also, many see this king as a type of a future Antichrist who will first make a covenant with the Jews – and then turn against them. As Bible-believing Christians, we cannot accept any of these interpretations. On the basis of the historicist principle of interpretation, we believe that Daniel 8:9-14 refers to the great controversy between Christ and Satan. This is a spiritual battle between God's plan of salvation and the counterfeit system of the little horn.

Daniel Nine Excerpt

It is very important to note the link between Daniel 8 and 9, and the way Daniel 9 explains Daniel 8:14, and that Daniel 8 and 9 form a unit. So, when Gabriel re-appeared, Daniel recognized that this was the same person "whom I had seen in the vision at first (Daniel 8:21)." In his opening sentence to Daniel, he declared, "O Daniel, I have now come out to give you wisdom and understanding." Gabriel is now commissioned to "make this man understand the vision" of chapter 8. He had before, explained everything except verse 14, with its references to the cleansing of the sanctuary and to the 2300 evening-and-morning days. Daniel understood the cleansing of the sanctuary, but the 2300 days were perplexing to him. These are literal days? He hoped! or were they symbolic like the other items in Daniel 8:3-14, and like the days in Ezekiel 4:6? And if they refer to 2300 years, was God saying that the Tamid services at the Jerusalem Temple would not be restored for 2300 years? What about Jeremiah's prophecy of 70 years? Gabriel stated: "Seventy weeks of years are decreed concerning your people and your holy city, to finish the transgression, to put an end to sin, and to atone for iniquity, to bring in everlasting righteousness, to seal both vision and prophet, to anoint a most holy place" (Daniel 9:24). Gabriel had come to explain the 2300 days prophecy. He explained that 490 years were to be "cut" or "amputated" from the longer period. Inasmuch as 490 years cannot be "cut" away from 2300 literal days, which add up to less than 7 years, the solution is clear. The 2300 days are indeed symbolic and stand for 2300 actual years. In verse 25 he further explained, "know therefore and understand ... that from the going forth of the word to restore and build Jerusalem to the coming of an anointed one, a prince, there shall be seven weeks." They were three decrees; however, the third decree was issued to rebuild Jerusalem and the temple.

According to (Ezra 7:25, 26), Artaxerxes gave a decree to Ezra to rebuild Jerusalem. It was a decree given in the seventh year of Artaxerxes, which gave Jerusalem its legal birth. Can this decree be dated? Beyond a shadow of a doubt! According to the Jewish calendar, Ezra is reported to have arrived in Palestine in the fifth month of the seventh year of Artaxerxes's reign. It is very important to note that the Jewish months are numbered from Spring to Spring. Therefore, the fifth month in old Jerusalem fell somewhere between mid-July and mid-September on our calendar. This was the time in the late summer or early autumn of 457 B.C., and the decree was implemented soon afterward. The seven weeks (49 years) from 457 B.C. brings us to 408 B.C., seventy weeks (490 years) from the autumn of 457 B. C., brings us to A.D. 34. Counting one week (7 years) back from A.D. 34 brings us to A.D. 27. Counting forward again 3 and a half years brings us to A.D. 31.

This biblical text of Daniel 9:25-27 is nestled deep in the most Christ-centered chapters of the Old Testament. Many Bible scholars believe that this biblical text of Daniel 9:25-27, when linked to Daniel 7:9-14 and Daniel 8:13-14, dates the judgment which precedes the second coming of Christ. For studies of Daniel chapter seven to chapter nine, shows that we are living in the hour of judgment. We are individually being declared safe in the den of lions by the blood of the Lamb of God. We are being rescued from the den of lions even today. "For God so loved the world, that He gave His only begotten Son, that whosoever believeth in Him should not perish, but have everlasting life. (John 3:16).

As we peruse Daniel nine, the chapter presents itself into three divisions. The first division is Daniel's "diary" referencing his study of the writings of Jeremiah (verse 1-3). He was very troubled and concerned about the scriptural text listed in Daniel 8:14, and its symbolic prediction, "unto two thousand and three hundred days; then shall the sanctuary be cleansed." Daniel had good reasons to know that it referred to the spiritual restoration or "cleansing" associated with the annual Day of Atonement. He had known Jeremiah the prophet during his childhood in Jerusalem. He unwrapped his cherished copy of Jeremiah's writings and read that after seventy years God would "punish the king of Babylon and the Chaldeans for their iniquity" (Jeremiah 25:11-12). He was excited, Babylon was already overthrown by the Medes and Persians, and Jerusalem had been subjugated for sixty-eight years. The seventy years were almost at an end! However, Jerusalem and its temple were in ruins; and nothing was being done to rebuild it. Can Jeremiah be wrong? Would the sanctuary lie waste for 2300 days? He reread the passage, "For thus says the Lord: When seventy years are completed for Babylon, I will visit you, and I will fulfill to you my promise, and bring you back to this place. For I know the plans I have for you, says the Lord....... And I will bring you back to the place from which I sent you into exile (Jeremiah 29:10-14). I am so happy; I can imagine Daniel's joy! These were, "Beautiful words, Wonderful words, Wonderful words of life, Beautiful words, Wonderful words, Wonderful words of life."

The second division is Daniel's prayer, and he prayed, and he prayed. As observed, most of Daniel nine consists of his prayer. The Bible is replete with prayer., but prayer like this can possibly give Satan a conscience. Daniel went into "fasting" and the use of "sackcloth and ashes" (Daniel 9:3). Daniel confessed his sins and the sins of Israel and ask for forgiveness for his people so that they can be released from captivity, and the restoration of the sanctuary can be a reality. He first confessed on behalf of his people (Daniel 9:3-6). He acknowledged that shame belongs to Israel but forgiveness belongs to God (Daniel 9:7-9). He acknowledged that Israel is in exile because of their transgressions (v 10-15). Then finally, he pleads for God's anger to be turned away (v 16-19). Daniel knew that God is a "covenant-keeping" God, a God who keeps His promises. So, at the beginning of his prayer, he addressed God as the ONE who "keepest covenant and steadfast love with those who love Him and keep His commandments" (Daniel 9:4). God cares! Prayer is power! Prayer brings deliverance!

It is important to reiterate that Daniel 2 gives us a panoramic view of the rise and fall of nations, and reaches its climax as Jesus, as the supernatural stone, establishes His kingdom of glory. As we look at Daniel 7, it takes us through the political scenes again, including the tragic course of medieval Christianity, and reaches its climax as the judgment is set in heaven, where Christ receives His Kingdom and graciously shares it with every saint found worthy.

The tent-sanctuary, or tabernacle, which God directed Moses to build, teaches us a whole lot about the Heavenly Sanctuary. Only priests were allowed into the Holy Place, and only the high priest, was allowed one day a year to enter the most Holy Place. The Day of Atonement dealt with the removal of sin, ceremonially from the sanctuary and from the people. The Day of Atonement is a day of judgment, and the cleansing of the sanctuary in Daniel 8:14 is closely parallel to the judgment scene of Daniel seven and to the arrival of the supernatural stone in Daniel two.

After the Israelites settled in Palestine, the tabernacle became worn and battered. Therefore, King Solomon replaced it with a stone temple in Jerusalem, based on the same basic plan as the worn tabernacle. It was this temple (Solomon's Temple) which Nebuchadnezzar razed to the ground more than three hundred years later. Soon after the Babylonian exile, the Jews built a second temple on the same principle, on the same spot as Solomon's Temple. This second temple did not contain the ark of the covenant, which hadn't been seen after Nebuchadnezzar's final attack.

The sanctuary rituals which God required were impressive and varied. They symbolized Christ's death and heavenly ministry for the forgiveness of our sins; according to the death of valuable animals, and the service of dedicated priests. The basic ritual was the offering of a lamb each morning and evening. It is recognized that God Himself miraculously kindled the fire for the Altar (Leviticus 9:24), when the tabernacle was originally dedicated. The priests were under strict instructions never to let it out. "This is the law of the burnt offering. The burnt offering shall be on the hearth upon the altar all night until the morning, and the fire of the altar shall be kept burning on it …. It shall not go out" (Leviticus 6:8-13).

The Lamb was offered twice a day; and in the New Testament, Jesus is often called a Lamb, the Lamb "which taketh away the sins of the world" (John 1:29; 1 Peter 1:19). Also, the cross of the New Testament, shows that Jesus could serve both as our Lamb and as our High Priest because He returned to life after the crucifixion. No lamb or bull or goat could illustrate the resurrection! However, God required the Levitical priests to perform a variety of rituals, because no single routine could adequately convey all the fullness of the gospel. The blood had to be applied from a variety of rituals, some of the blood from every sacrifice made for sin, was sprinkled on or near one of the two Altars. "It is the blood that makes atonement" (Leviticus 17:11). However, Christ "entered once for all into the Holy Place, taking His blood ... His own blood, thus securing an eternal redemption" (Hebrews 9:12).

We know that the Old Testament Tamid was important to God. He instituted it, and He was concerned that Antiochus Epiphanes would interrupt it briefly and that the Roman Empire would contribute to its demise. As the metals, beasts, and horns of Daniel's prophecies, which are symbols of empires and kingdoms, so is the Tamid of Daniel 8:13-14 a symbol. It is a symbol of the continual ministry of Jesus Christ in the Heavenly Sanctuary, forgiving of our sins and providing power for us to live changed lives in fulfillment of the new covenant promise.

The purpose for the Day of Atonement was the removal of sin, ceremonially from the sanctuary and truly from the people. Through Moses, God told the Israelites that the high priest entered the most holy place not only to "make atonement for the sanctuary" but also to make atonement "for you, to cleanse you," so that "from all your sins you shall be clean before the Lord" (Leviticus 16:30-33). The Day of Atonement being a day of judgment, we sense immediately that the cleansing of the sanctuary in Daniel 8:14 is closely parallel to the judgment scene of Daniel seven and to the arrival of the supernatural stone in Daniel two. The judgment in Daniel seven compares readily with the entry of Christ as High Priest into heaven's most holy place at the commencement of the celestial Day of Atonement or Day of Judgment. Daniel eight is the sanctuary being purified from, (1) the attack of the little horn, and (2) the record of sins of the saints. Hence the "books being opened" in Daniel seven, and everyone who was found described in the Book (Daniel 12:1-2) being rescued. The Book points back to the record of sins in the sanctuary in Lev.16. That record was cleansed on the Day of Atonement. So, it is a twofold cleansing, (1) from the doctrinal errors of the papacy, and (2) from the character errors of the saints.

Daniel Ten Excerpt

It is clearly evident that we are in a battle – a battle of good over evil, of God and Satan. It is the greatest conflict of all times, playing out from the beginning of creation to this time of the end. The devil knows that his time is short, and he is up to his old tricks (Revelation 12:12). We need to pray earnestly and never give up. We need to pray more than ever than before asking God to send His strongest angels to stand guard over us. We are aware of the Prince of Persia as mentioned in (Daniel 10:20), an angel-prince who identified himself with the Persian Empire. A demonic entity, an angel under Satan who withstood the Angel Gabriel for "twenty-one days; but Michael, one of the chief princes, came to help" him (verse 13). It took Christ Himself, in assisting the Angel Gabriel for him to get the upper hand in this battle. This is a serious situation that should be preached in every pulpit around the world. Imagine a fallen angel withstanding the Angel Gabriel for three weeks! We must conclude that it was a really intense struggle with supernatural beings of power lock in a battle to save the nation of Persia. We are ever thankful that the angels of God, are more than able. Second Peter 2:4 tells us of angels who sinned and were cast out of heaven. Therefore, this could have been a powerful fallen angel. Paul states, that the gods that the nations worshiped were in reality angels (1 Corinthians 10:20). Therefore the "prince of Greece," similarly is an evil angel. Obviously, they are still doing the same today, to bring about Satan's evil scheme. One of the singularly most important verses in scripture, Daniel 10, verse 13, dramatizes the battle, and the invisible powers and spiritual influences on nations in the world. It is heartening to know though, that spiritual beings are constantly on the march carrying out God's purpose in this world of sin to defend His people (Exodus 12:23; 2 Samuel 24:16), and in the moral world as well (Luke 15:10).

Daniel Eleven Excerpt

In this "time of the end," any comment, especially coming from the President of the United States that appears to lend credence of any kind to the idea of an ID or mark before you can buy or sell, will obviously send shivers up the spine of many, and cause those who follow prophecy closely to exclaim, "we told you so!" On July 31st, 2018, President Donald Trump stated at a Tuesday night rally in Tampa, Florida, "You know, if you go out and you want to buy groceries, you need a picture on a card, you need ID. You go out and you want to buy anything, you need ID and you need your picture," in a rally to drum up support for GOP Rep. Ron DeSantis' gubernatorial bid. This is the original quote from the President of the United States, the leader of the free world. He was giving his support for tougher ID requirements for voters. Can this be considered normal speech? Even normal political campaigning? For an accomplished person of great authority and influence, to easily throw such words around, it just can be possible that countries like ours can have demonic entities assigned. It is quite possible that these demonic entities are at play in influencing the attack on the mailing of bombs to influential individuals, other major catastrophes such as the Tree of Life Synagogue. Here is the description in poetry format!

Tree of Life: In Terror and In Hope

— In memory and solidarity of the Pittsburgh "Tree of Life Synagogue" shooting victims —

9:45 AM, 46, 47, 48, 49, 50, 51, 52, 53, 9:54 AM

In the shattering of time
Hell danced as the bullets chimed
Bullets and Pulpits war
Pulpits and Bullets war
A mystical madness replaced all praise
Wallowing only in one phrase
Bullets and Pulpits war
Pulpits and Bullets war
Writing in death
Slaying and taking breath
Hope can catch no star
Hope can catch no star.

Eleven dead
From bullets of hate
Six more hit and bled
In terror and in hope.

In the shattered peace
The finger of death issued another increase
Bullets wading, cutting piece by piece
Ripping hearts and taking life
Sowing hate and sowing strife
Wrapped itself like a statue on the mind
Where is the love that bought mankind
In this wicked reality
Lies an American Tragedy.

Eleven dead
From bullets of hate
Six more hit and bled
In terror and in hope.

In the early October morn
And the midmorning of its dawn
Bullets whizzed in terror
Bringing ultimate horror
Can hope live in Pittsburgh still
In the heart of Squirrel Hill
In the heart of America, where bullets kill, and kill, and kill, and kill,
and kill, and kill, and kill, and kill, and kill, and kill, and kill!

Eleven dead
From bullets of hate
Six more hit and bled
In terror and in hope.

End.

Tree of Life Continued

In Maxwell's interpretation of the "king of the north" and "king of the south," he explains that – after Alexander's kingdom was divided at his death – the far west went to Cassander, the North to Lysimachus, the East to Seleucus, and the south to Ptolemy. Also, this term appears frequently in Daniel 11. The names apply to the rulers who controlled Syria and Egypt: countries lying north and south of Jerusalem. However, the actual areas of these kings vary from time to time.

The northern (Seleucid) kingdom sometimes reached from the Aegean Sea to India, and sometimes consists of only a few city-states. The king of (Ptolemaic) Egypt carried the name Ptolemy – and all the kings of Syria who are referred to in Daniel 11 were called either Antiochus or Seleucus. Thereafter, the Roman state was succeeded by the Roman Church – that is, the "Augustus" was succeeded by the "Holy Father". The "contemptible person", then the medieval pope, rose in the place of Augustus; verses 25-30 of Daniel 11 foreshadow the crusades. The Muslims controlled Jerusalem at the time of the first crusade and held control from time to time. They were headed by the Caliphs or Sultans in Egypt. Therefore, the first crusade was a great attack against the "king of the south" (Daniel 11:24-25). It was a great success for the king of the north over the king of the south when Jerusalem was brutally overtaken. It was the papacy who bore the primary responsibility for the crusades and their ghastly atrocities. In contrast, Doukhan was clear that the whole chapter of Daniel 11 speaks to the little horn power or, more precisely, the papacy. He sees the Roman Empire only mentioned in the phrase "Alexander's kingdom shall be plucked up" and given to others (Rome).

In studying the Book of Daniel, the content of my prayers has undergone a drastic change. I now ask God to send His angels to stand guard over our country, our leaders, over me and my family, my friends, my acquaintances, and His very elect. This is my continual prayer.

Daniel Twelve Excerpt

In evaluating the "king of the north" and the "king of the south," the main message can be found in Daniel 11, which states, "And at that time of the end shall the king of the south push at him: and the king of the north shall come against him like a whirlwind, with chariots, and with horsemen, and with many ships; and he shall overflow and pass over. He shall enter also into the glorious land, and many countries shall be overthrown but these shall escape out of his hand, even Edom, and Moab, and the chief of the children of Ammon. He shall stretch forth his hand also upon the countries: and the Land of Egypt shall not escape. But he shall have power over the treasurers of gold and of silver, and over all the precious things of Egypt: and the Libyans and the Ethiopians shall be at his steps." We are aware that the "king of the north" is the papacy and actually can be discussed as Satan himself, coming at "the end of time", impersonating Christ to deceive the people – causing many to worship on Sunday instead of on the seventh-day Sabbath. The "king of the south" is of Egypt. Obviously, the "king of the north" has lots of deceptive power. There are many differing views out there, but it is biblical that the papacy is the king of the north, and Egypt is the "king of the south." As we come upon the end of time, at the time of the end, it's time to praise and shout; for Christ Jesus is the victory. He is the Alpha and Omega, throughout time: throughout history. He reigns, He reigns forever and ever and ever.

According to Maxwell, Daniel chapter 12:11-12, the Angel speaks of 1290 days and of the blessedness of a person who waits to the end of 1335 days. The Angel does not provide an event for the close of the 1290 days, and neither for the beginning or end of the 1335 days. The estimated time is when the Roman Church became the harlot, by relying on the power of the kings of the earth, rather than Christ's power. This is the reasoning for the beginning of the 1335 days because there is no specific event to point to, or mentioned about its beginnings. However, the implications are that it began at the same time as the 1290 days. If this is so, the 1335 days ended in 1883 or 1884 (Supplement 12 A: "Daniel and His Interpreters.").

The time has come for all of us with this last day message to "let the cat out of the bag," and be even more assertive, to boldly proclaim, by sharing in every way possible, on every social media and every media platform, the three angels' message of (Revelation 14:6-12), to show the urgency to every nation, and kindred, and tongue and people, that they need to worship God and keep His Sabbath Holy. We must let the world know today we need to Fear God, to Give Him all the Glory, and to Worship Him! For "if any man worship the beast and his image, and receive his mark in his forehead, or in his hand, the same shall drink of the wine of the wrath of God." We are very fortunate to be able to serve God in our churches, temples and synagogues basically uninterrupted so far until these major shootings taking place and this major covid-19 pandemic. These are probably a precursor to the impending doom that will be unleashed against those who worship on the Sabbath. We are fortunate that we still have time in giving basically uninterrupted worship at our designated places weekly by way of in person or on zoom and other online platforms, to continue worshiping a loving God, who has given us free will. We are free to serve Him or to oppose Him. In Daniel 12:1, Michael is here introduced as "the great prince" who has charge of God's people. In Revelation 12:7-9, we find a similar picture, where Michael and his angels fought the prince of evil and his angels. Yet the outcome in both books is the same; Michael, the great prince, overcomes Satan and delivers his people. We are literally in a war zone. The Devil is marshaling his forces, and Michael is directing the defense of His people. Unlike nations parading their missiles ready to attack, the Devil is already on the attack. Obviously, the Devil has ambassadors in every country, state, and city. I'm in total agreement that he has princes in the cities of the world. We are fortunate to have Michael the Archangel: the Prince of Peace.

SECTION II

–

Daniel 1

"In the third year of the reign of Jehoiakim king of Judah came Nebuchadnezzar king of Babylon unto Jerusalem, and besieged it. And the Lord gave Jehoiakim king of Judah into his hand, with part of the vessels of the house of God: which he carried into the land of Shinar to the house of his god; and he brought the vessels into the treasure house of his god. And the king spake unto Ashpenaz the master of his eunuchs, that he should bring certain of the children of Israel, and of the king's seed, and of the princes; Children in whom was no blemish, but well favoured, and skilful in all wisdom, and cunning in knowledge, and understanding science, and such as had ability in them to stand in the king's palace, and whom they might teach the learning and the tongue of the Chaldeans. And the king appointed them a daily provision of the king's meat, and of the wine which he drank: so nourishing them three years, that at the end thereof they might stand before the king. Now among these were of the children of Judah, Daniel, Hananiah, Mishael, and Azariah: Unto whom the prince of the eunuchs gave names: for he gave unto Daniel the name of Belteshazzar; and to Hananiah, of Shadrach;

and to Mishael, of Meshach; and to Azariah, of Abed-nego. But Daniel purposed in his heart that he would not defile himself with the portion of the king's meat, nor with the wine which he drank: therefore he requested of the prince of the eunuchs that he might not defile himself. Now God had brought Daniel into favour and tender love with the prince of the eunuchs. And the prince of the eunuchs said unto Daniel, I fear my lord the king, who hath appointed your meat and your drink: for why should he see your faces worse liking than the children which are of your sort? then shall ye make me endanger my head to the king. Then said Daniel to Melzar, whom the prince of the eunuchs had set over Daniel, Hananiah, Mishael, and Azariah, Prove thy servants, I beseech thee, ten days; and let them give us pulse to eat, and water to drink. Then let our countenances be looked upon before thee, and the countenance of the children that eat of the portion of the king's meat: and as thou seest, deal with thy servants. So he consented to them in this matter, and proved them ten days. And at the end of ten days their countenances appeared fairer and fatter in flesh than all the children which did eat the portion of the king's meat. Thus Melzar took away the portion of their meat, and the wine that they should drink; and gave them pulse. As for these four children, God gave them knowledge and skill in all learning and wisdom: and Daniel had understanding in all visions and dreams. Now at the end of the days that the king had said he should bring them in, then the prince of the eunuchs brought them in before Nebuchadnezzar. And the king communed with them; and among them all was found none like Daniel, Hananiah, Mishael, and Azariah: therefore stood they before the king. And in all matters of wisdom and understanding, that the king inquired of them, he found them ten times better than all the magicians and astrologers that were in all his realm. And Daniel continued even unto the first year of king Cyrus." (Daniel 1).

Where Is Your God? Allowing the Prophet Daniel to Speak

— "That bringeth the princes to nothing; maketh the judges of the earth as vanity" — Isaiah 40:23

Even though impaled by the bondage of time
Exiled and trapped in walls; I'm confined!
Left in the bosom of a new race
Ripples of selfishness, caught in a maze, confused and dazed!
Yet my heart shall steadfastly rest on Jehovah-Rapha
For God is my only hope, my God and Savior!
In the dark nights of my experience
And the sinful days of indifference!
Whilst my heart cries out in total fear
Though some look at God as being austere
His eternal love to me is totally clear!
Lord! Let me stand like the brave
Hooked and locked to you through Jesus your Son whom you gave!
Though the whole world is in utter turmoil
And your mightiness: the enemy tries to foil!
Blood bought, sanctified am I – and God alone anointed my head
with oil! with oil! (Romans 8:31-32; Psalm 23:5)

Exiled to Babylon from the land of Palestine
I speak and write my rhyme
Though taken from the Kingdom of Judah
My heart shall steadfastly rest on Jehovah-Rapha
Daniel or Belteshazzar, or whatever name's bestowed
I pledge to honor the God to whom all I owed
In the fearsome nights or in the terrible days
Go fan the flames or stoke the blaze!
I'll stand like I'm brave or kneel in reverential prayer!
For my God is more than able to deliver!

The world had taken a tacit turn
The Assyrian Empire was gone
And now the newest world power ruled, called Babylon
Known as the land of the mighty Chaldeans
A land of many historic scenes
Which Nimrod the mighty hunter founded (Genesis 10)
The site where the well-known Tower of Babel was erected
(Genesis 11)
Where men were in common language, and proudly conscripted
To challenge the God who enthroned on high
Who created man from the very dust, and to whom the breath of
life supplied!
There where the famous lawmaker Hammurabi reigned
Even before Moses' exit from Egypt, and Israel's exodus fame
For God has always been in the affairs of men
From the time of creation: unto the coming for His children
And always honor those who served Him well
Allowing Christ Jesus to go to the cross: to save mankind from hell
To whom His holy angels visited, and to whom His Holy Spirit
dwelt

In open-hearted love: God rides on the clouds in search: for
Mankind, His heart melts!
God promised, that in due time, men will prophesy again!
And Daniel's verses will be understood at "the time of the end!"

For the God who brought us to this trial
Promised to take us through it yet: and restore the temple defiled
King Nabopolassar furnished his son, the crown prince
Nebuchadnezzar with an army
Who defeated the Egyptians, and captured territory!
And subjected Judah to penalty!
At his father's death, Nebuchadnezzar became king
And ruler over everything!

King Nebuchadnezzar sacked and pillaged the land of Judah thrice
Taken us into captivity: but Jeremiah's prophetic words again recite
And hid in our hearts
That though from Canaan's dear and happy land we depart
Our steps in Jerusalem, be indelibly marked
So, in the days in Babylon, no foe, or wine, nor rich food can
conspire
'Cause to serve our God is our only desire
So, we beg of you chief eunuch Ashpenaz
Give to us a vegetarian diet, the test we'll pass
Of the consequences, we know you're afraid
But our resolve is true: do not feel betrayed

Oh, steward! Grant to us a ten-day trial
The result will be worthwhile
And finally, at the end of ten days, our mind's most versatile and
true!

We stood before Nebuchadnezzar the King, yes, we did: all the
world knew!
Then appointed to his government with great privilege: we did
endure!

From the days of the kingdom of Babylon
In the experience of great feats: and great phenomenon
In momentous times: and sometimes glorious!
Unto the age of Medio-Persia: of the anointed one: king Cyrus!
The Lord God Jehovah reigns: with agape love enfolding us!

End.

Reflections

Herein, we find Daniel and his friends separated from those they love most and the things they know, like safety in the care of their parents and familiar surroundings of their hometown. This poetic writing focuses on the human chaotic conditions and emotions, coming out of the tragic history of the conquest of Judah. It is quite relatable to many situations in our world today when life takes us through the twists and turns and lands us distressed or celebrating. In familiarizing yourself with this biblical story, you will begin to appreciate this poetic exposé and its import.

The beauty of this work is in its imagery from history and coining it to be applicable for us today. The word "pledge" used in the poetic structure, implies entering into a covenant relationship. I challenge you to read and reread, to find the beauty in this poetic journey, and to find your God. We're reminded to talk to God about what we experience through our sensory perception as He (GOD) is the one who is truth. Who is Man to challenge God's authority? Although life throws us curve-balls most times, and we are disappointed sometimes, we are challenged to rest on His unchanging hands (Romans 8:35). For God's promises are sure.

Chapter 1 Prayer

My God, I stand a captive of circumstances and of my sins. Yet my heart glory in you! For you are a forgiving and delivering God. Forgive me, please change the vicissitudes of my life, and gift to me a new trajectory. Let me glory in your majesty and delivering power. Let the blood that was shed on Calvary, reach my sin-sick soul, reach me in my dark hour, and save me from this bondage of sin. In Jesus' name. Amen.

Personal Reflections

_____

_____

_____

_____

_____

_____

_____

_____

_____

Daniel 2

"And in the second year of the reign of Nebuchadnezzar Nebuchadnezzar dreamed dreams, wherewith his spirit was troubled, and his sleep brake from him. Then the king commanded to call the magicians, and the astrologers, and the sorcerers, and the Chaldeans, for to shew the king his dreams. So they came and stood before the king. And the king said unto them, I have dreamed a dream, and my spirit was troubled to know the dream. Then spake the Chaldeans to the king in Syriack, O king, live for ever: tell thy servants the dream, and we will shew the interpretation. The king answered and said to the Chaldeans, The thing is gone from me: if ye will not make known unto me the dream, with the interpretation thereof, ye shall be cut in pieces, and your houses shall be made a dunghill. But if ye shew the dream, and the interpretation thereof, ye shall receive of me gifts and rewards and great honour: therefore shew me the dream, and the interpretation thereof. They answered again and said, Let the king tell his servants the dream, and we will shew the interpretation of it. The king answered and said, I know of certainty that ye would gain the time, because ye see the thing is gone from me. But if ye will not make known unto me the dream, there is but one decree for you: for ye have prepared lying and corrupt words to speak before me, till the time be changed: therefore tell me the dream, and I shall know that ye can shew me the interpretation thereof. The Chaldeans answered before the king, and said, There is not a man upon the earth that can shew the king's matter: therefore there is no king, lord, nor ruler, that asked such things at any magician, or astrologer, or Chaldean. And it is a rare thing that the king requireth, and there is none other that can shew it before the king, except the gods, whose dwelling is not with flesh. For this cause the king was angry and very furious, and commanded to destroy all the wise men of Babylon. And the decree went forth that the wise men should be slain; and they sought Daniel and his fellows to be slain. Then Daniel answered with counsel and wisdom to Arioch the captain of the king's guard, which was gone forth to slay the wise men of Babylon: He answered and said to Arioch the king's captain, Why is the decree so hasty from the king? Then Arioch made the thing known to Daniel. Then Daniel went in, and desired of the king that he would give him time, and that he would shew the king the interpretation. Then Daniel went to his house, and made the thing known to Hananiah, Mishael, and Azariah, his companions: That they would desire mercies of the God of heaven concerning this secret; that Daniel and his fellows should not perish with the rest of the wise men of Babylon. Then was the secret revealed unto Daniel in a night vision. Then Daniel blessed the God of heaven. Daniel answered and said, Blessed be the name of God for ever and ever: For wisdom and might are his: And he changeth the times and the seasons: He removeth kings, and setteth up kings: He giveth wisdom unto the wise, And knowledge to them that know understanding: He revealeth the deep and secret things: He knoweth what is in the darkness, And the light dwelleth with him. I thank thee, and praise thee, O thou God of my fathers, Who hast given me wisdom and might, And hast made known unto me now what we desired of thee: For thou hast now made known unto us the king's matter. Therefore Daniel went in unto Arioch, whom the king had ordained to destroy the wise men of Babylon: he went and said thus unto him; Destroy not the wise men of Babylon: bring me in before the king, and I will shew unto the king the interpretation. Then Arioch brought in Daniel before the king in haste, and said thus unto him, I have found a man of the captives of Judah, that will make known unto the king the interpretation. The king answered and said to Daniel, whose name was Belteshazzar, Art thou able to make known unto me the dream which I have seen, and the interpretation thereof? Daniel answered in the presence of the king, and said, The secret which the king hath demanded cannot the wise men, the astrologers, the magicians, the soothsayers, shew unto the king; But there is a God in heaven that revealeth secrets, and maketh known to the king Nebuchadnezzar what shall be in the latter days. Thy dream, and the visions of thy head upon thy bed, are these; As for thee, O king, thy thoughts came into thy mind upon thy bed, what should come to pass hereafter: and he that revealeth secrets maketh known to thee what shall come to pass. But as for me, this secret is not revealed to me for any wisdom that I have more than any living, but for their sakes that shall make known the interpretation to the king, and that thou mightest know the thoughts of thy heart. Thou, O king, sawest, and behold a great image. This great image, whose brightness was excellent, stood before thee; and the form thereof was terrible. This image's head was of fine gold, his breast and his arms of silver, his belly and his thighs of brass, His legs of iron, his feet part of iron and part of clay. Thou sawest till that a stone was cut out without hands, which smote the image upon his feet that were of iron and clay, and brake them to pieces. Then was the iron, the clay, the brass, the silver, and the gold, broken to pieces together, and became like the chaff of the summer threshingfloors; and the wind carried them away, that no place was found for them: and the stone that smote the image became a great mountain, and filled the whole earth. This is the dream; and we will tell the interpretation thereof before the king. Thou, O king, art a king of kings: for the God of heaven hath given thee a kingdom, power, and strength, and glory. And wheresoever the children of men dwell, the beasts of the field and the fowls of the heaven hath he given into thine hand, and hath made thee ruler over them all. Thou art this head of gold. And after thee shall arise another kingdom inferior to thee, and another third kingdom of brass, which shall bear rule over all the earth. And the fourth kingdom shall be strong as iron: forasmuch as iron breaketh in pieces and subdueth all things: and as iron that breaketh all these, shall it break in pieces and bruise. And whereas thou sawest the feet and toes, part of potters' clay, and part of iron, the kingdom shall be divided; but there shall be in it of the strength of the iron, forasmuch as thou sawest the iron mixed with miry clay. And as the toes of the feet were part of iron, and part of clay, so the kingdom shall be partly strong, and partly broken. And whereas thou sawest iron mixed with miry clay, they shall mingle themselves with the seed of men: but they shall not cleave one to another, even as iron is not mixed with clay. And in the days of these kings shall the God of heaven set up a kingdom, which shall never be destroyed: and the kingdom shall not be left to other people, but it shall break in pieces and consume all these kingdoms, and it shall stand for ever. Forasmuch as thou sawest that the stone was cut out of the mountain without hands, and that it brake in pieces the iron, the brass, the clay, the silver, and the gold; the great God hath made known to the king what shall come to pass hereafter: and the dream is certain, and the interpretation thereof sure. Then the king Nebuchadnezzar fell upon his face, and worshipped Daniel, and commanded that they should offer an oblation and sweet odours unto him. The king answered unto Daniel, and said, Of a truth it is, that your God is a God of gods, and a Lord of kings, and a revealer of secrets, seeing thou couldest reveal this secret. Then the king made Daniel a great man, and gave him many great gifts, and made him ruler over the whole province of Babylon, and chief of the governors over all the wise men of Babylon. Then Daniel requested of the king, and he set Shadrach, Meshach, and Abed-nego, over the affairs of the province of Babylon: but Daniel sat in the gate of the king." (Daniel 2).

Wisdom and Might: Nebuchadnezzar's Dream

— "The fear of the Lord is the beginning of knowledge: but fools despise wisdom and instruction" — Proverbs 1:7

Have seen my visions: Have dreamt my dreams
Have walked in the steps of Daniel: with leaders of glittering
schemes
Of iron: of clay: of bronze: the silver and the golds
I've seen my Shadrachs: my Meshachs: my Abednegos
The days of dreams aren't gone: Or over: or over!
In these weary last days of time: my heart has discovered
As God has promised: sons and daughters will prophesy
This is the time to testify: this is the time to prophesy!
This is my testimony
Of God and me: my story: my destiny
Let me tell you the story of daughters and sons: of daughters and of
sons: of daughters and of sons
For the glory of the moon will wane: the brightness will fade of the
sun
For God will reign in the hearts of the children
God will reign on Mount Zion: Jerusalem

His glory shall reign among men
And young men will see visions: and old men will dream dreams
(Acts 2:17)
The devil and his angels: will try his devilish schemes
And you and I: will stand like Daniel: at this time of the end!
You and I: we will prophesy again! (Revelation 10:10-11)

King Nebuchadnezzar of Babylon, had a dream in the second year
of his reign
That he could not remember, or even explained
He summoned all the fortune-tellers, to tell him the dream
Regardless though, they couldn't gleam it or even schemed.
The king became angry and furious and decreed death
Yet, divine connection took the executioner to Daniel's steps
Daniel asked Arioch, "why is the decree so severe?"
The captain sought to make it clear
Then, Daniel went in to see the king and pleaded for time
Oh, what a paradigm!
Prophetically designed!

Daniel went to his home
But not to commune with God alone
He must recall the dream and its interpretation.
Pleading for mercy with Hananiah, Mishael, and Azariah until it's
revealed
To servants of God, nothing is concealed!
As the mystery was revealed in a vision of the night
They praised and thank God, to whom belongs wisdom and might!
For God alone, brings what is in darkness
into light!

Then Daniel rushed into Arioch, where he was stationed
"Do not destroy the wise men of Babylon, take me to the king
I will show him the interpretation!
In they rushed, and Arioch announced to the king
"I found this exile who can make known everything.
Then Nebuchadnezzar asked, "can you make known the dream and
its interpretation?"
Daniel spoke under the threat of death and condemnation
No wise men, Daniel said can: "but there is a God who reveals
mysteries
Only to you: God has made known the future of the world, and its
destiny!
Oh, king – you saw a great mighty image, immensely bright
It was frightening in the light.
The head of the image was of fine gold
Its breast and arms of silver, therein enfold
Its belly and thighs of bronze, like something to behold
Its legs of iron, so profoundly cold
Its feet partly of iron, partly of clay, so majestic and bold
But: as you looked, a stone cut out by no human hand
In the dream of Nebuchadnezzar: Time to understand
Smote the image on its feet of iron and clay!
And there it lay!

Then the iron, the clay, the bronze, the silver, and the gold
All became chaff, on the summer's threshing floor
And the wind carried them away
Away without a trace, this is no hearsay
But: the stone that struck the image!
Became a great mountain and filled the whole earth with full
privilege!

In this impressive dream, here is the interpretation, the true story
The God of Heaven has given you King Nebuchadnezzar a
kingdom, power, might, and glory!
You are the head of gold: this is what the dream foretold
Then shall arise another kingdom inferior to you
This is the silver kingdom, it's not all about you.
And yet another kingdom of bronze shall rule over the Earth
Along came the fourth kingdom, unlike any other, and of much
worth
Strong as iron, shattering, breaking, and crushing
Isn't that amazing!
Still this kingdom
With feet and toes, of partly clay and partly iron!
Even though mixed in marriage: will never cleave together long!

The stone you saw, cut from a mountain with no human hand
This you must understand!
In the days of those kings, the God of heaven will set up a Kingdom
It shall never be destroyed, God will reign with majesty, power, and
dominion!
It shall break to pieces, the gold, the silver, the bronze, and the iron
And forever, and ever, and ever stand
For the dream is certain, and its interpretation sure!
For JESUS is the precious cornerstone, who endures!
(Isaiah 28:18; Luke 20:17-18)

King Nebuchadnezzar did homage and gave to Daniel gifts
Fulfilling all of Daniel's wish
Made him ruler over the land, and the wise men of Babylon
Appointing Shadrach, Meshach, and Abednego over the affairs of
the land

All because of the God of gods he finally knew!
This is the end of the story of Daniel two!

End.

Reflections

There are many leaders in this world, past and present today, who are consumed by their authority, and the trappings of power. Several of them of varying authority, offer up decrees that are detrimental to their constituents, clients, and members. Also, not only leaders of a country or a state but even of organizations, businesses, CEOs of companies, managers, and even the moral bastions of society – our synagogues, temples, mosques, mandirs, and churches. Some of these exercise wanton power over those they perceive as being inferior and they themselves superior. It all resides in their ego and the unfulfilled need to control or to be recognized. Some may bellow from the top of their voices that you have to obey their rules because this is their country, state, church, synagogue, mosque, or temple. They fail to recognize that it is God who established everything and give them authority and power. They fail to recognize that no power can prevail against God's church, the gates of hell shall not prevail against it! (Matthew 16:18).

However, the ruler of a country presides with more overarching power that can be used to cause utter distress, greater harm, and death. Despite it all, Daniel was a stalwart in leadership who showed himself trustworthy to a heathen king whose vexatious spirit was ready to decree death at every step. When executing his faith, Daniel solicits the prayers of his like-minded friends, as not to presume victory all to himself. Therefore, I urge you to appreciate this poetic artistry and beauty in retelling the most wonderful historic prophecy of all time. The word "mighty" gives a connotation of being fearsome, remarkable, powerful, and extraordinary.

It is only a true and living God that could speak through his prophet; in demonstrating His true and awesome power. We find Daniel walking by faith, the utmost transforming faith, even unto the threat of death. Even today, with the help of God, one's voice can affect change for the better, despite all the odds in one's life and the things that are besetting the world. My challenge to you is to find the beauty expressed in this poetry; in finding the beauty, may you find your God.

Chapter 2 Prayer

Father and God, please forgive me of all my wrongs and gift to me a victor's song. Let my prayer ascend like sweet incense into your presence. For strongholds need to be broken. Dreams need to be interpreted and fulfilled. Lives need to be saved. My life is in danger and needs to be saved. The whole world is imperiled. Danger on all sides but you are in charge! No one can change the future, a future you have foretold. Draw us just a little closer oh Lord and deliver, deliver and deliver. For your name's sake. Amen.

Personal Reflections

_____

_____

_____

_____

_____

_____

_____

_____

Daniel 3

"Nebuchadnezzar the king made an image of gold, whose height was threescore cubits, and the breadth thereof six cubits: he set it up in the plain of Dura, in the province of Babylon. Then Nebuchadnezzar the king sent to gather together the princes, the governors, and the captains, the judges, the treasurers, the counsellers, the sheriffs, and all the rulers of the provinces, to come to the dedication of the image which Nebuchadnezzar the king had set up. Then the princes, the governors, and captains, the judges, the treasurers, the counsellers, the sheriffs, and all the rulers of the provinces, were gathered together unto the dedication of the image that Nebuchadnezzar the king had set up; and they stood before the image that Nebuchadnezzar had set up. Then an herald cried aloud, To you it is commanded, O people, nations, and languages, That at what time ye hear the sound of the cornet, flute, harp, sackbut, psaltery, dulcimer, and all kinds of musick, ye fall down and worship the golden image that Nebuchadnezzar the king hath set up: And whoso falleth not down and worshippeth shall the same hour be cast into the midst of a burning fiery furnace. Therefore at that time, when all the people heard the sound of the cornet, flute, harp, sackbut, psaltery, and all kinds of musick, all the people, the nations, and the languages, fell down and worshipped the golden image that Nebuchadnezzar the king had set up. Wherefore at that time certain Chaldeans came near, and accused the Jews. They spake and said to the king Nebuchadnezzar, O king, live for ever. Thou, O king, hast made a decree, that every man that shall hear the sound of the cornet, flute, harp, sackbut, psaltery, and dulcimer, and all kinds of musick, shall fall down and worship the golden image: And whoso falleth not down and worshippeth, that he should be cast into the midst of a burning fiery furnace. There are certain Jews whom thou hast set over the affairs of the province of Babylon, Shadrach, Meshach, and Abed-nego; these men, O king, have not regarded thee: they serve not thy gods, nor worship the golden image which thou hast set up. Then Nebuchadnezzar in his rage and fury commanded to bring Shadrach, Meshach, and Abed-nego. Then they brought these men before the king. Nebuchadnezzar spake and said unto them, Is it true, O Shadrach, Meshach, and Abed-nego, do not ye serve my gods, nor worship the golden image which I have set up? Now if ye be ready that at what time ye hear the sound of the cornet, flute, harp, sackbut, psaltery, and dulcimer, and all kinds of musick, ye fall down and worship the image which I have made; well: but if ye worship not, ye shall be cast the same hour into the midst of a burning fiery furnace; and who is that God that shall deliver you out of my hands? Shadrach, Meshach, and Abed-nego, answered and said to the king, O Nebuchadnezzar, we are not careful to answer thee in this matter. If it be so, our God whom we serve is able to deliver us from the burning fiery furnace, and he will deliver us out of thine hand, O king. But if not, be it known unto thee, O king, that we will not serve thy gods, nor worship the golden image which thou hast set up. Then was Nebuchadnezzar full of fury, and the form of his visage was changed against Shadrach, Meshach, and Abed-nego: therefore he spake, and commanded that they should heat the furnace one seven times more than it was wont to be heated. And he commanded the most mighty men that were in his army to bind Shadrach, Meshach, and Abed-nego, and to cast them into the burning fiery furnace. Then these men were bound in their coats, their hosen, and their hats, and their other garments, and were cast into the midst of the burning fiery furnace. Therefore because the king's commandment was urgent, and the furnace exceeding hot, the flame of the fire slew those men that took up Shadrach, Meshach, and Abed-nego. And these three men, Shadrach, Meshach, and Abed-nego, fell down bound into the midst of the burning fiery furnace. Then Nebuchadnezzar the king was astonied, and rose up in haste, and spake, and said unto his counsellers, Did not we cast three men bound into the midst of the fire? They answered and said unto the king, True, O king. He answered and said, Lo, I see four men loose, walking in the midst of the fire, and they have no hurt; and the form of the fourth is like the Son of God. Then Nebuchadnezzar came near to the mouth of the burning fiery furnace, and spake, and said, Shadrach, Meshach, and Abed-nego, ye servants of the most high God, come forth, and come hither. Then Shadrach, Meshach, and Abed-nego, came forth of the midst of the fire. And the princes, governors, and captains, and the king's counsellers, being gathered together, saw these men, upon whose bodies the fire had no power, nor was an hair of their head singed, neither were their coats changed, nor the smell of fire had passed on them. Then Nebuchadnezzar spake, and said, Blessed be the God of Shadrach, Meshach, and Abed-nego, who hath sent his angel, and delivered his servants that trusted in him, and have changed the king's word, and yielded their bodies, that they might not serve nor worship any god, except their own God. Therefore I make a decree, That every people, nation, and language, which speak any thing amiss against the God of Shadrach, Meshach, and Abed-nego, shall be cut in pieces, and their houses shall be made a dunghill: because there is no other God that can deliver after this sort. Then the king promoted Shadrach, Meshach, and Abed-nego, in the province of Babylon." (Daniel 3).

Fiery Furnace: Image of Gold/Symbolic Image

The Three Hebrew Boys

— **"When thou passest through the waters, I will be with thee; and through the rivers, they shall not overflow thee: when thou walkest through the fire, thou shall not be burned; neither shall the flame kindle upon thee."— Isaiah 43:2**

The language of the head of gold or the language of the symbolic
image
Cannot make my heart be dismayed, for I will press towards the
mark of the blessed and privileged
Nebuchadnezzar's image of pure gold
Cannot break my spirit, cannot break my hold
For on the solid rock of Christ I stand, strong and bold
I will worship no image nor serve no other gods in Babylon
Like Shadrach, Meshach and Abednego, heat the furnace seven
times. Let it burn! Let it burn!
The burning fiery furnace may raze!
Like a new structure in Christ, I'll rise, the world to amaze

No decree of death, no mystical spell, can keep me in the fire!
Dance the flames, call the blaze – Man will live and not expire
Stoke the blaze; know you not that Christ, Jesus, still inspires! (Psalm
91)

King Nebuchadnezzar made an image of gold
Whose height in cubits was 60, approximately 90 feet or threescore
Its breath in cubits 6, the story is told
So profoundly impressed was he by the gold-headed image he had
dreamt
His puffed-up heart sought to circumvent
Nebuchadnezzar proposed his image to surpass any ever seen
The image must surpass the one in his dream
He would make an image of gold from head to toe
None must compare to Babylon; the whole world must know!
Taller than the towering statues of Egypt
A challenge to the Tower of Babel – image of gold must be
strategic!
All must come to worship it, on the pain of death
This is not a simple threat; it is a decree. It is to be worshipped – or
death!
He set it up in Dura's plains, in the province of Babylon, for all to
behold
The land of the head of gold, foreshadowing the symbolic image; 'tis
Nebuchadnezzar's image of pure gold! (Revelation 13)

King Nebuchadnezzar gathered together
The princes and governors to come hither
The captains, the judges, and treasurers
The sheriffs, and counselors
Commanding all of Babylon and the rulers

To gather them all together
At the dedication of the image
One nation uniting in worship as one village!
Worshipping the image, that the king had set up!
This was not a fake lineup or a fake mix-up; Nebuchadnezzar was
the big bishop!
The herald cried aloud, commanding all people, nations, and
languages
That at the sound of the music: worship! or you will suffer more
than punitive damages!
The coronet, flute, harp, sackbut, psaltery, and all kinds of music
sound
To worship the golden image: all the people of the nations and
languages fell down!
Prostrating themselves in reverential worship on the ground
For whosoever falleth not down and worship not will be cast into
the fiery furnace!
None will be spared, none who disobeyed: Wipe the scourge from
off the earth, an utter disgrace
Wipe away the menace! (Revelation 17:6)

The Chaldeans accused the Jews who did not fall down to worship
Seizing the opportunity, where grudgeful heart portends hardship
Accosting the king with their diatribe
Oh, great king Nebuchadnezzar – live forever, your lordship
You made the decree that all should fall down and worship!
At the sound of the cornet, flute, harp, sackbut, psaltery, dulcimer,
and all kind of music
All must fall down in total reverence the golden image to worship!
Yet, there are certain Jews you set over the province of Babylon
They regard you not, worship not your gods, nor the golden image,

nor honor your command

According to your decree, any man who does not obey

Should be cast into the fiery furnace that very day!

Shadrach, Meshach, and Abednego regard thee no, serve not your god, nor the image you set up!

Nebuchadnezzar was enraged: "bring the Jews: bring them up!"

As they came, he asked: do you not serve my gods, nor worship the image, which I have set up?

Now, if you're ready,

At the sound of the music of the cornet, flute, harp, sackbut, dulcimer, and psaltery,

You shall fall down and worship the image which I have made

If you worship not and stop not this escapade

You will be cast into the fiery furnace!

And who is that God that can deliver you from my malice!

Shadrach, Meshach, and Abednego said to the king: we are not careful to answer

The God we serve is able to deliver!

Even from the burning fiery furnace; He will deliver us from your hands

Be it known, if not: we will never serve any gods, nor worship any golden image in Babylon's lands

Then Nebuchadnezzar, full of fury, mad like the devil, heated the furnace seven times more – he commanded it!

Bind them hand and foot, mighty men of mine; cast them into the furnace lit

Shadrach, Meshach, and Abednego were cast into the furnace

In their coats, hats, and other garments, into the midst of the burning fiery furnace

The flames of the furnace danced and slew the mighty men in the

King's service

Although Shadrach, Meshach, and Abednego fell bound into the
midst of the burning fiery furnace

The King was then astonished to see

four men loose in the burning fiery furnace totally free!

He rose and asked his counselors – didn't we cast three?

They concurred: that's true

Nebuchadnezzar declared that the fourth man was like the Son of
God; he knew!

Then he came near to the mouth of the burning fiery furnace and
shouted

He spoke and shouted: come out, come out!

Shadrach, Meshach, and Abednego

Servants of the living God, come hither; thanks be to the God you
know! (2 Samuel 22:2-3)

They came out from the burning fiery furnace of hell

With the princes, governors, captains, and the king's counselors all
gathered, like in a magical spell!

Mystified that the fire had no power

Mystified that not even one hair on their heads suffered!

Nor the smell of smoke consumed or devoured!

For the burning fiery furnace killed the mighty men of valor; of the
King, Nebuchadnezzar, just remember. Just remember!

So, Nebuchadnezzar praised and blessed the God of Shadrach,
Meshach, and Abednego that day

Thanking God for the deliverance of His trusted servants who'd
never betray!

Nebuchadnezzar ordered and decreed that no one should of the God
of Heaven speak ill

'Cause they shall be cut into pieces, their houses made into dunghills

For there is no other God that can deliver in that way
And Nebuchadnezzar promoted Shadrach, Meshach, and Abednego
that very day! (James 5:13–16)

End.

Reflections

The image you project is an extension of your good or bad thoughts and intentions. To influence others to follow your dictates, by making a physical image and ordering them to worship it, is by extension worshiping the one who created it, which is a reflection of a mad, egotistical, conceited, and insipid mindset or a dictatorial attitude. It is a characteristic of Satan, the one that motivates such an individual. This was the situation in which Shadrach, Meshach, and Abednego found themselves in the presence of Nebuchadnezzar's wanton power.

It is good to have a sound self-image and in projecting it, you can transform and inspire others to be the best they can be. Therefore, the three Hebrew boys were able to stand in the face of Nebuchadnezzar's nonsense, because they were secured in their own image, and secured by the image of the God they worship. They were not confused about a fake substitute for the real image. They knew who they were and of whose they were. They were able to stand because they were accustomed to being different by virtue of their teachings from a young age. Although threats were heaped upon them, they decided to exercise their choice to worship the living God only. We must realize that we have a God-given power of choice and the support of the heavenly beings to assist us in living out our choice for Jesus. Remember that whomsoever Jesus sets free is free indeed and cannot be bound by the dictates of human dictatorship. We have the Holy Spirit who convicts the heart, causing us to worship only the God of the universe. The word here is, "image" staring back at us. God created man in His own image (Genesis 1:26-27). We need to stand for God because we are the image of God and the crowning act of His creative majesty (Psalm 8:3-8). I challenge you to look for the beauty and artistry flowing from this poetic work created from the Word of God Himself and be inspired to walk and worship God who created mankind in His own image.

Chapter 3 Prayer

Dear God, I'm on my knees again. First of all, cleanse me and forgive my sins. May you forgive the leaders of the nations of this world who do not see you but only see themselves. They cause others to worship the images that they set up. However, uplift and strengthen those that know your ways, and let your mercy remain with men a little longer, seal your children! Save us from our fiery furnaces, and make us steadfast in service of you. Save us all in the time of the end, for Christ Jesus' name's sake. Amen.

Personal Reflections

Daniel 4

"Nebuchadnezzar the king, unto all people, nations, and languages, that dwell in all the earth; Peace be multiplied unto you. I thought it good to shew the signs and wonders that the high God hath wrought toward me. How great are his signs! and how mighty are his wonders! his kingdom is an everlasting kingdom, and his dominion is from generation to generation. I Nebuchadnezzar was at rest in mine house, and flourishing in my palace: I saw a dream which made me afraid, and the thoughts upon my bed and the visions of my head troubled me. Therefore made I a decree to bring in all the wise men of Babylon before me, that they might make known unto me the interpretation of the dream. Then came in the magicians, the astrologers, the Chaldeans, and the soothsayers: and I told the dream before them; but they did not make known unto me the interpretation thereof. But at the last Daniel came in before me, whose name was Belteshazzar, according to the name of my god, and in whom is the spirit of the holy gods: and before him I told the dream, saying, O Belteshazzar, master of the magicians, because I know that the spirit of the holy gods is in thee, and no secret troubleth thee, tell me the visions of my dream that I have seen, and the interpretation thereof. Thus were the visions of mine head in my bed; I saw, and behold a tree in the midst of the earth, and the height thereof was great. The tree grew, and was strong, and the height thereof reached unto heaven, and the sight thereof to the end of all the earth: The leaves thereof were fair, and the fruit thereof much, and in it was meat for all: the beasts of the field had shadow under it, and the fowls of the heaven dwelt in the boughs thereof, and all flesh was fed of it. I saw in the visions of my head upon my bed, and, behold, a watcher and an holy one came down from heaven; He cried aloud, and said thus, Hew down the tree, and cut off his branches, shake off his leaves, and scatter his fruit: let the beasts get away from under it, and the fowls from his branches: Nevertheless leave the stump of his roots in the earth, even with a band of iron and brass, in the tender grass of the field; and let it be wet with the dew of heaven, and let his portion be with the beasts in the grass of the earth: Let his heart be changed from man's, and let a beast's heart be given unto him; and let seven times pass over him. This matter is by the decree of the watchers, and the demand by the word of the holy ones: to the intent that the living may know that the most High ruleth in the kingdom of men, and giveth it to whomsoever he will, and setteth up over it the basest of men. This dream I king Nebuchadnezzar have seen. Now thou, O Belteshazzar, declare the interpretation thereof, forasmuch as all the wise men of my kingdom are not able to make known unto me the interpretation: but thou art able; for the spirit of the holy gods is in thee. Then Daniel, whose name was Belteshazzar, was astonied for one hour, and his thoughts troubled him. The king spake, and said, Belteshazzar, let not the dream, or the interpretation thereof, trouble thee. Belteshazzar answered and said, My lord, the dream be to them that hate thee, and the interpretation thereof to thine enemies. The tree that thou sawest, which grew, and was strong, whose height reached unto the heaven, and the sight thereof to all the earth; Whose leaves were fair, and the fruit thereof much, and in it was meat for all; under which the beasts of the field dwelt, and upon whose branches the fowls of the heaven had their habitation: It is thou, O king, that art grown and become strong: for thy greatness is grown, and reacheth unto heaven, and thy dominion to the end of the earth. And whereas the king saw a watcher and an holy one coming down from heaven, and saying, Hew the tree down, and destroy it; yet leave the stump of the roots thereof in the earth, even with a band of iron and brass, in the tender grass of the field; and let it be wet with the dew of heaven, and let his portion be with the beasts of the field, till seven times pass over him; This is the interpretation, O king, and this is the decree of the most High, which is come upon my lord the king: That they shall drive thee from men, and thy dwelling shall be with the beasts of the field, and they shall make thee to eat grass as oxen, and they shall wet thee with the dew of heaven, and seven times shall pass over thee, till thou know that the most High ruleth in the kingdom of men, and giveth it to whomsoever he will. And whereas they commanded to leave the stump of the tree roots; thy kingdom shall be sure unto thee, after that thou shalt have known that the heavens do rule. Wherefore, O king, let my counsel be acceptable unto thee, and break off thy sins by righteousness, and thine iniquities by shewing mercy to the poor; if it may be a lengthening of thy tranquillity. All this came upon the king Nebuchadnezzar. At the end of twelve months he walked in the palace of the kingdom of Babylon. The king spake, and said, Is not this great Babylon, that I have built for the house of the kingdom by the might of my power, and for the honour of my majesty? While the word was in the king's mouth, there fell a voice from heaven, saying, O king Nebuchadnezzar, to thee it is spoken; The kingdom is departed from thee. And they shall drive thee from men, and thy dwelling shall be with the beasts of the field: they shall make thee to eat grass as oxen, and seven times shall pass over thee, until thou know that the most High ruleth in the kingdom of men, and giveth it to whomsoever he will. The same hour was the thing fulfilled upon Nebuchadnezzar: and he was driven from men, and did eat grass as oxen, and his body was wet with the dew of heaven, till his hairs were grown like eagles' feathers, and his nails like birds' claws. And at the end of the days I Nebuchadnezzar lifted up mine eyes unto heaven, and mine understanding returned unto me, and I blessed the most High, and I praised and honoured him that liveth for ever, whose dominion is an everlasting dominion, and his kingdom is from generation to generation: And all the inhabitants of the earth are reputed as nothing: and he doeth according to his will in the army of heaven, and among the inhabitants of the earth: and none can stay his hand, or say unto him, What doest thou? At the same time my reason returned unto me; and for the glory of my kingdom, mine honour and brightness returned unto me; and my counsellers and my lords sought unto me; and I was established in my kingdom, and excellent majesty was added unto me. Now I Nebuchadnezzar praise and extol and honour the King of heaven, all whose works are truth, and his ways judgment: and those that walk in pride he is able to abase." (Daniel 4).

In the Midst of Earth

— Herein lies the judgment: Herein lies the truth —
— "Where no counsel is, the people fall: but in the multitude of
counselors there is safety." — (Proverbs 11:14)

Let me write a poem or write a song
Of how men and rulers, both young and strong
With selfish hearts and wickedness, can never call first on God
Embracing things demonic and not the Lord
Like King Saul's secret encounter with the woman of Endor
Talking to spirits of the dead. Remember the Devil is a big
pretender
The dead are dead; the dead cannot praise the Lord
For, in death, you return to the Earth, the breath to God (Psalm
115:17, Psalm 146:4)
No other gods – magicians, astrologers, soothsayers – are of any
special worth
This is just a timely reminder, a timely alert
A change must come; the heart is a golden thing
Only repentance from sin can make a life sing
Once again, Nebuchadnezzar had to be schooled
How many times can a man be a fool?

Like I may think, I'm all that
You may think you're a bureaucrat
And bigger, bigger than Nebuchadnezzar's tree
Just remember: God is bigger, bigger than any decree, bigger than
you, and bigger than me
God can make you a stumped root
He declares His judgments; God doesn't look at how you're cute
God looks at the truth
His blessings are unmatched, flowing like the fountain
God Almighty does as He will in the army of heaven
And in the world of men
Loving and forgiving
Go tell your daughters, go tell your sons, go tell your friends
God giveth rulership to whomsoever He wills
God giveth rulership to the basest of men, though bereft of moral
courage, compassion, and skills!

In this most amazing proclamation: made around 569 BC by
Nebuchadnezzar
Of God's leading in his life: after 35 years on the throne: he declared
in great measure
Unto all people, nations, and languages upon the whole earth
It's incumbent to show the wonder-working power of God at work
For great are His signs and mighty are His wonders!
Splitting the heart that sins asunder like fearsome thunder
His dominion is from generation unto generation; His kingdom is
everlasting and none can counter!
The great Nebuchadnezzar was at the top of his game, then he had
another dream!
His heart failed him; he shouted and screamed
It made him so afraid and very troubled

Once again, he decreed and brought all the wise men on the double
Fear of death rested upon the dream interpreter's interpretation
The magicians, the astrologers, the Chaldeans, and the soothsayers
came – but were afraid and in hesitation
Then, at last, Daniel – now a friend – known as Belteshazzar came
in whom dwelt the spirit of the living God
The dream was outlined in all its graphic detail to the famed
interpreter from Judah
Although Nebuchadnezzar remembered the dream, the wise men
hesitated in its interpretation
But Daniel listened in utter consternation!

Oh Daniel, oh Belteshazzar!
Exclaimed Nebuchadnezzar
Master of the magicians, endowed with the spirit of the living God,
that nothing troubleth thee
Hear my troubling dream and reveal the interpretation to me!
The dream occurred as he laid contented, on his bed
With the whole world at his feet, yet he dreads
For Nebuchadnezzar had seen a magnificent tree in the midst of the
earth
The tree grew; the height was great and strong from birth
The height of the tree, though, reached heaven – and its sight over
the world
With leaves that fair, with much fruit for all
Giving safety to the beast of the field
In it, the birds of heaven securely shielded and all flesh fed on its feed
Then a watcher from heaven, a holy one,
Exclaimed, with a loud shouted command,
Crying out aloud: "Hew down the tree!"
Now, to roam deserted like an animal, 'tis the destiny

Cut off his branches, shake off his leaves, scatter his fruits of plenty
Chase the beast from under it, chase the birds from his branches,
then leave a stump of his root in the earth
This is really going to hurt!
Now put a band of iron and brass around the stumped root
Herein lies the judgment; herein lies the truth
This is the complete declaration, wet with the dew of heaven
Let his dwelling be – with the beasts, in the grass of the Earth, even
With a heart that changed from a man's to that of a beast
Seven times shall pass over him; his reign must cease!
This is decreed by the watchers and the demand of the holy ones
For all must know that the Most-High God ruleth in the kingdom
of men – go tell your daughters, go tell your sons!
God giveth rulership to whomsoever He wills
And gives leadership even to the basest of men though bereft of
moral courage, compassion, and skills!

Nebuchadnezzar saw and remembered the dream
The wise men couldn't give the interpretation; they didn't even try
nor even schemed
Daniel, able and capable, came – for the spirit of the living God
dwelt in him
Still, Daniel was astonished for one hour; words fled from him!
Although the interpretation he instantly knew – in his heart bled an
intense struggle
He was very distressed and troubled!
The king urged him not to be – just tell the interpretation; be
comfortable
It's time to understand, it's time for destiny
This was pain in complexity!
In the interpretation of this dream

Daniel declared to the king: let the dream be to them that hate you
and your enemies; this interpretation was very extreme!
The tree which you saw, whose height was great and strong from
birth
With the height of it reaching heaven and its sight over the world
With leaves that fair and with much fruit for all
Which gave safety to the beasts of the field
Where the birds of heaven were securely shielded
Wherein all flesh fed on its feed
The tree is a representation of you, King Nebuchadnezzar
For you have grown and are now strong – your greatness has now
risen to heaven afar
Your dominion over the ends of the world
Your power over the world unfurled
And where you saw a watcher coming down from heaven, a holy
one
Who exclaimed, in a loud shouted command!
Crying out aloud: "Hew down the tree!"
So, to roam deserted like an animal, 'tis the destiny
Cut off his branches, shake off his leaves, scatter his fruits of plenty
Chase the beasts from under it, chase the birds from his branches.
Then, leave a stump of his root in the earth
This is really going to hurt!
Put a band of iron and brass on the stumped root
Herein lies the judgment; herein lies the truth
This is the complete declaration: wet with the dew of heaven
Let his dwelling be, with the beasts, in the grass of the Earth – even
With a heart that changed from a man's to that of a beast
Seven times shall pass over him; his reign must cease
This is decreed by the Most-High God to Nebuchadnezzar the king

This is the interpretation of everything
They shall drive you away from men; your dwelling shall be with
the beasts
Certainly, most certainly, your reign must cease
You shall eat grass as an ox with oxen
This is the complete declaration: wet by the dew of heaven
Your judgement shall be for the years of seven
The world must know – that God Almighty ruleth in the kingdom
of men
Go tell your daughters, go tell your sons, go tell your friends
God giveth rulership to whomsoever He wills
And gave leadership even to the basest of men, though bereft of
moral courage, compassion, and skills!

For as to the command to leave the stump in the earth rooted
With a band of iron of brass, left grounded,
The kingdom shall be sure when repented
Nebuchadnezzar was counseled: break off your sin
Away with iniquity; show mercy to the poor; let peace and love
begin
Change your destiny – write a new song of history
But for one full year, he held no fear; what a tragedy
For he spoke about his majesty and what he had built
Great Babylon: head of gold; land of filth
Then he was driven out, without any guilt
He dwelt as an animal with the beasts of the field, ate the grass like
oxen, even forgot what he was
His hairs grew like eagle's feathers; his nails like birds' claws
Nebuchadnezzar, wet with the dew of heaven, ate grass for seven
years
Until he acknowledged that the God of heaven is to be feared!

That the Most-High God ruleth in the kingdom of men
And to whomsoever He wills, He assigns rulership and befriends
When Nebuchadnezzar lifted up his eyes to heaven in worship
Suddenly, his understanding returned; the decree fled, all the
hardship!
His song exclaimed: all the inhabitants of the world are as nothing
Blessings unmatched, flowing like a fountain!
God Almighty, do as He wills in the army of heaven
Loving and forgiving
God Almighty, do as He wills, among the inhabitants of the Earth
His blood was shed on Calvary's dirt
His dominion is from generation to generation, His kingdom is
everlasting and none can counter
Nebuchadnezzar was blessed with the return of his glory, kingdom,
and honor!
The darkness drifted; brightness returned – excellent majesty,
counselors, and lords
Now Nebuchadnezzar praised, extolled – honor the King of
Heaven, as God! as God! as God!
King of kings and Lord of lords!

End.

Reflections

When faced with adverse situations beyond our control, many of us do not seek God first for guidance and help. Instead, some of us go to unfamiliar spirits to get answers. We allow our pride to take control, until late in the game when some of us may come to realize that only God can move the mountains with which we find ourselves confronted. There is a phrase that is regularly used, but it's rooted in Proverbs 16:18, "pride goeth before destruction, and a haughty spirit before a fall." For us to be drawn closer to God, we have to divest ourselves of pride to gain victory.

We should note how merciful God is and appreciate the warning given to Nebuchadnezzar from God before He acted upon his life as a means of correction. If we can only heed God's warning, only then we will be able to catch a glimpse of what God truly desires for our lives. To catch this vision, we need to surrender to God. To truly appreciate the message in this chapter, you must read the interweaving chapters of Daniel and delve into the other books from Genesis to Revelation. The word or words here are stumped roots. Does they live? How is it possible that in something that seems dead there may be life? Obviously, God didn't totally dig out the stump but left it in a rooted position. It is clear that the God we serve is a

God of second chances. Although pride caused a great king to fall and go insane to teach him a life lesson, it was only temporarily inflicted on him on the basis of God's specific instructions. God has the final say over your life and it's your choice to listen to Him. Within this poetic text, the poet emphasizes the illusory presence of Lucifer, the great pretender, who will be bound by circumstances for one thousand years. Look around deeper into this poetic work, find the prophetic and the magnificence of God.

Chapter 4 Prayer

Loving Lord, mighty are your wonders. Your dominion is from generation to generation and your kingdom is everlasting. May your name be glorified in all the earth. Forgive our sins and draw us closer to you. Let the darkness drift away and your glory fill our souls. In Jesus' name. Amen.

Personal Reflections

_____

_____

_____

_____

_____

_____

_____

_____

_____

Daniel 5

"Belshazzar the king made a great feast to a thousand of his lords, and drank wine before the thousand. Belshazzar, whiles he tasted the wine, commanded to bring the golden and silver vessels which his father Nebuchadnezzar had taken out of the temple which was in Jerusalem; that the king, and his princes, his wives, and his concubines, might drink therein. Then they brought the golden vessels that were taken out of the temple of the house of God which was at Jerusalem; and the king, and his princes, his wives, and his concubines, drank in them. They drank wine, and praised the gods of gold, and of silver, of brass, of iron, of wood, and of stone. In the same hour came forth fingers of a man's hand, and wrote over against the candlestick upon the plaister of the wall of the king's palace: and the king saw the part of the hand that wrote. Then the king's countenance was changed, and his thoughts troubled him, so that the joints of his loins were loosed, and his knees smote one against another. The king cried aloud to bring in the astrologers, the Chaldeans, and the soothsayers. And the king spake, and said to the wise men of Babylon, Whosoever shall read this writing, and shew me the interpretation thereof, shall be clothed with scarlet, and have a chain of gold about his neck, and shall be the third ruler in the kingdom. Then came in all the king's wise men: but they could not read the writing, nor make known to the king the interpretation thereof. Then was king Belshazzar greatly troubled, and his countenance was changed in him, and his lords were astonied. Now the queen, by reason of the words of the king and his lords, came into the banquet house: and the queen spake and said, O king, live for ever: let not thy thoughts trouble thee, nor let thy countenance be changed: There is a man in thy kingdom, in whom is the spirit of the holy gods; and in the days of thy father light and understanding and wisdom, like the wisdom of the gods, was found in him; whom the king Nebuchadnezzar thy father, the king, I say, thy father, made master of the magicians, astrologers, Chaldeans, and soothsayers; Forasmuch as an excellent spirit, and knowledge, and understanding, interpreting of dreams, and shewing of hard sentences, and dissolving of doubts, were found in the same Daniel, whom the king named Belteshazzar: now let Daniel be called, and he will shew the interpretation. Then was Daniel brought in before the king. And the king spake and said unto Daniel, Art thou that Daniel, which art of the children of the captivity of Judah, whom the king my father brought out of Jewry? I have even heard of thee, that the spirit of the gods is in thee, and that light and understanding and excellent wisdom is found in thee. And now the wise men, the astrologers, have been brought in before me, that they should read this writing, and make known unto me the interpretation thereof: but they could not shew the interpretation of the thing: And I have heard of thee, that thou canst make interpretations, and dissolve doubts: now if thou canst read the writing, and make known to me the interpretation thereof, thou shalt be clothed with scarlet, and have a chain of gold about thy neck, and shalt be the third ruler in the kingdom. Then Daniel answered and said before the king, Let thy gifts be to thyself, and give thy rewards to another; yet I will read the writing unto the king, and make known to him the interpretation. O thou king, the most high God gave Nebuchadnezzar thy father a kingdom, and majesty, and glory, and honour: And for the majesty that he gave him, all people, nations, and languages, trembled and feared before him: whom he would he slew; and whom he would he kept alive; and whom he would he set up; and whom he would he put down. But when his heart was lifted up, and his mind hardened in pride, he was deposed from his kingly throne, and they took his glory from him: And he was driven from the sons of men; and his heart was made like the beasts, and his dwelling was with the wild asses: they fed him with grass like oxen, and his body was wet with the dew of heaven; till he knew that the most high God ruled in the kingdom of men, and that he appointeth over it whomsoever he will. And thou his son, O Belshazzar, hast not humbled thine heart, though thou knewest all this; But hast lifted up thyself against the Lord of heaven; and they have brought the vessels of his house before thee, and thou, and thy lords, thy wives, and thy concubines, have drunk wine in them; and thou hast praised the gods of silver, and gold, of brass, iron, wood, and stone, which see not, nor hear, nor know: and the God in whose hand thy breath is, and whose are all thy ways, hast thou not glorified: Then was the part of the hand sent from him; and this writing was written. And this is the writing that was written, MENE, MENE, TEKEL, UPHARSIN. This is the interpretation of the thing: MENE; God hath numbered thy kingdom, and finished it. TEKEL; Thou art weighed in the balances, and art found wanting. PERES; Thy kingdom is divided, and given to the Medes and Persians. Then commanded Belshazzar, and they clothed Daniel with scarlet, and put a chain of gold about his neck, and made a proclamation concerning him, that he should be the third ruler in the kingdom. In that night was Belshazzar the king of the Chaldeans slain. And Darius the Median took the kingdom, being about threescore and two years old." (Daniel 5).

Tragedy From Within

— Babylon found wanting: 'tis Babylon's time
— "Heaven and earth shall pass away, but my words shall not
pass away" — Matthew 24:35

Let me declare today and every day
Let me confess and speak to say
God is worthy of our praise
God the Father, God the Son, God the Holy Spirit still amaze!
In calling everything into existence, the heaven and the earth
To the crown of creation, forming man from the very dirt
When the Earth was without form and void, and darkness covered it
all
From the east, west, north, and south, God issued a command, an
ultimate call
As the Almighty God moves upon the face of the waters, in the
mystery of the trinity – in trinity of power (John 14:1)
God said: "Let there be light" – and light appeared, not a minute late
nor in an hour
He saw the light was good and divided the light from the darkness
Where there is light, God should be worshipped, ignorance
harnessed

116

For despite the unrivaled love of God
Declaring the jealousness of the Lord
Today, the hand of judgment is writing on the wall
Today, this is a final call
How can your heart be lifted up and hardened with pride?
Against the One who gave His Son who died?
And flaunt one's self, testing the patience of God
How can you wrestle against the Lord?
MENE, MENE, TEKEL, UPHARSIN
MENE, MENE, TEKEL, UPHARSIN
MENE, MENE, TEKEL, UPHARSIN
God has numbered your kingdom and finished it –
Our life is in it; our life is in it!
We are weighed in the balances and are found wanting
Call on God – His love is like a living fountain
Judgment has come to you, on your own; you can do nothing
Run to God, claim the blood that Jesus shed!
He is alive who once was dead
Your kingdom is now divided and given
To the Medes and the Persians
Run from the enemy. God is your refuge. God is your potion
Your potion and salvation. Your potion and salvation (Psalm 73:26;
142:5)

King Belshazzar of Babylon: son of Nabonidus, grandson of
Nebuchadnezzar, the dreamer
Hosted a grand feast in honor of a thousand of his lords and civic
leaders
This was on October 12th, 539 BC. With their wives and mistresses
all in attendance,
Wine flowed; spirits rose. Reality became blurred, ego reached the

sky, lost in a mystical dance
Reality became a game. Women plus power; power plus women;
man plus circumstance!
Romance and abundance
Abundance and romance
Bad timing and planning – time to understand
Tragedy from within Babylon!
Now, Babylon had suffered much – since Nebuchadnezzar's death,
twenty-three years before
His incompetent son then reigned: evil Merodack, murdered by his
brother-in-law; a settled score (Jeremiah 52:31-34; 2 Kings
25:27-30)
The brother-in-law Nergalsharezer/Neriglassar then claimed the
throne of Babylon (Jeremiah 39:3, 13)
He died four years later, leaving his minor son
The minor son Laborosoarchod, taken from the throne and killed
So Nabonidus, the father of King Belshazzar, reigned until
He was then taken to worship the moon god called sin
What a great calamity: death and wickedness; wickedness and death;
tragedy after tragedy – tragedy from within!
The priests couldn't stand his worship of sin – the neglect of the
Babylonian patron god Marduk: apostasy and sin
They couldn't stand his theology; they couldn't stand his testifying
Nabonidus as king did no celebrating
Babylon in distress; Babylon suffering. Babylon suffering!
No New Year's celebration for ten long years
Financial recession, labor gangs; Babylon was in tears!

Meanwhile, Cyrus the great – the Persian king
Empowered, anointed, overpowering
Captured the kingdom of Media and Lydia

Nabonidus, alarmed at the empowered Persian power, rushed back
to Babylon in 540 BC from Tema
Still, though, he couldn't muster popular support
Went up against the forces of Cyrus on October 10th, 539 BC –
then surrendered the city of Sippar, in the north. Lack of fight, lack
of thought
In a quick flight, Nabonidus fled south to the city of Borsippa
Whilst Babylon left unguarded with his son the feasting Belshazzar!
The march of the silver kingdom was on – Darius the Mede moved
rapidly south to Babylon
Babylon, head of gold. Babylon – oh, Babylon
Tragedy from within, enemy at the door
Babylon found wanting – 'tis Babylon's time, Babylon of evil and
the poor!
From within, the feast was on – wine, women, and song
Judgment must come: a cleansing of wrong!
Belshazzar then commanded: bring the vessels of gold and silver
The sacred vessels, taken from the temple of Jerusalem by
Nebuchadnezzar
That his wives, mistresses, and concubines might drink therein
Vessels from the temple of God, servants brought them all for the
king
Then the king, his princes, his wives, and his concubines drank their
wine
In praise to the gods of gold, of silver, of brass, of iron, of wood, and
of stone – where wickedness cannot confine!
In that same hour came the finger of a man's hand
Time to plan; time to understand
The hand wrote over against the candlesticks
Upon the plaster of the wall of bricks

In the palace of Belshazzar, the king – he saw the part of the hand
that wrote
His countenance changed; a troubled heart. His loins were loosed,
his knees knocked and smote!
Then he cried aloud: bring the astrologers, the Chaldeans, and the
soothsayers
And he said: whosoever shall read this writing and tell the
interpretation shall receive all favors
He shall be clothed with scarlet, with a chain of gold around his
neck and crowned third ruler of Babylon
Still, all the king's wise men could not read the writing nor tell the
interpretation
King Belshazzar was greatly troubled; the lords were astonished!
Then the queen–mother entered and by reason of her words said to
the king – she admonished –
"Oh king, live forever: let not your thoughts troubled thee, nor your
countenance be changed"
There is a man in your kingdom in whom is the spirit of the living
God – your life can be rearranged
For in the days of your father, light, understanding, and wisdom –
like the wisdom of God – was found in him
In the days of your father, Nebuchadnezzar, I state again – your
father, the king,
He made Daniel name Belteshazzar master of the magicians,
astrologers, Chaldeans, and soothsayers. Stop being grim – just call
on him
Daniel was brought before the King
And was asked: aren't you a captive from Judah of the land of the
Jews?
I found out, as I did my reviews

It is spoken. And I've heard that the spirit of God dwelleth in you:
light, understanding, And excellent wisdom
As you can see, Daniel, the wise men, the astrologers, have been
brought in before me; we must save the kingdom
They came to read the writing and make known their
interpretations to me
Yet they couldn't show the interpretation thereof; 'tis a sad day, we
must agree!
The story is told – that you can make interpretations and dissolve
doubts
If you read the writing and give the interpretation thereof. Babylon
will celebrate and Babylon will shout
Then, you will receive all favors
You shall be clothed with scarlet, with a chain of gold around your
neck, and crowned third ruler of Babylon. It's now or never!
Daniel answered: "let your gifts be to yourself and give your reward
to another"
Yet will I read the writing and give the interpretation
For the Most-High God gave your father Nebuchadnezzar a
kingdom and majesty, and glory, and honor
And for the majesty he received, all people, nations, and languages
feared before him, and stood under his banner
He slew whom he would, kept alive whom he would set up, and
whom he would he put down with his awesome power
Then his heart was lifted up. His mind hardened with pride, he was
deposed from his throne and they took his glory
As he was driven from the sons of men; his heart was made like a
beast's and he dwelt with the animals of the field, though transitory
Ate grass like oxen, wet with the dew of heaven, until he
acknowledged that God Almighty ruled in the kingdom of men.

This is the story
And you who knew this Belshazzar – humble not your heart
Yet, you lifted up yourself against the Lord of Heaven, even from
the start
Brought the vessels of His temple before you: your lords, your
wives, your concubines – you're an upstart!
From the vessels, you drunk wine; this kingdom is ripped apart!
Praising the gods of silver, of gold, of brass, iron, wood and stone
Which see not, nor hear, nor know
Feasting like the devil – God's greatest foe
And the God whom giveth your breath who has kept you in all your
ways, you have not glorified, nor giveth no praise!
God is disgusted and has weighed you in your ways
Therefore, was the part of the hand sent from God – and this
writing was written Comprehend it!
"This is the writing that's written: MENE, MENE, TEKEL,
UPHARSIN
This is the interpretation of the thing: MENE., God has numbered
your kingdom and finished it"
"TEKEL, you are weighed in the balances and are found wanting"
Judgment has come. You can do nothing
"PERES, your kingdom is divided and given to the Medes and
Persians"
So is the Aramaic word "Parsin", plural for "Peres"; in it, no
contradictions
Kingdom of breast and arm of silver, or the lopsided bear, or the
unequal, high horns of the ram (Daniel 2, Daniel 7, Daniel)
These were the grim realities of Babylon
Overcome by the Medes and the Persians
While the feasting and banqueting ensued, they diverted the waters

of the Euphrates. The river
Entered Babylon, slewed the guards, and killed Belshazzar
We have crested on history and the faith of Man
What is there not to understand!
Babylon the kingdom is no more – time for the Medes and time for
Persians!

End.

Reflections

This epic poem coming out of this very familiar story from Daniel 5, reflects on the in-depth historical account of the rulers and the then king of Babylon. It highlights the systematic failure of this great kingdom, primarily due to pride and forgetfulness of the living God. We find the finger, intruding upon the party-goers in a very expressive way. It portends judgment and finality in the life of the nation, rulers of darkness, and those who partake of the defiling of the sacred vessels of God.

We can appreciate the poetics clearly as we see a crescendo of God's nearness from heaven to Earth as He was being ignored, mocked, disrespected; a perfect God in a quest to get the attention of imperfect humans. The finger of God writes a cryptic message on the wall; just above the live band members' heads to get everyone's attention. Yet God was patient and only let His hands be seen, with the movement interrupting the party-goers and the terrified king. What if God appeared fully, would they have all died on the spot? I can see God's mercy with just the entrance of His finger and the back of His hand. In deciphering the written words and giving them meaning, discernment was not given to anyone else in the kingdom, except Daniel. He was a trusted servant of God and the one who was accustom to interpreting messages from God to the earthly rulers. It's a clear demonstration of God showing that He rules over all rulers of the earth and their subjects.

King Belshazzar died that same night, most likely in a drunken state of mind without any chance of repentance for his behavior. The challenge is to remember God is a jealous God who will not just stand idly by without intervention. Sometimes there is a tragic end by the choices made, but your life does not have to end by death. By making the right decision you can receive the gift of salvation which is free. As the apostle John expounded, "If the Son, therefore, shall make you free, ye are free indeed." (John 8:36) The words, "Romance and abundance, abundance and romance," are beautifully inlaid, not only in text but in giving context to the situation at hand. I challenge you to find more beauty in this poetry. Be motivated to ultimately see the beauty of the character of God.

Chapter 5 Prayer

Father and God, forgive our stubborn and pompous hearts. The handwriting is on the wall of all the earth and the devil is at the door, come save us. When we look upon the things that are upon us, let us make the paradigm shift to sacredness. Let our bodies be the temple you so desire to dwell within and stop the desecration from within. This is my humble prayer, in Jesus' name. Amen.

Personal Reflections

_____

_____

_____

_____

_____

_____

_____

_____

_____

6

Daniel 6

"It pleased Darius to set over the kingdom an hundred and twenty princes, which should be over the whole kingdom; And over these three presidents; of whom Daniel was first: that the princes might give accounts unto them, and the king should have no damage. Then this Daniel was preferred above the presidents and princes, because an excellent spirit was in him; and the king thought to set him over the whole realm. Then the presidents and princes sought to find occasion against Daniel concerning the kingdom; but they could find none occasion nor fault; forasmuch as he was faithful, neither was there any error or fault found in him. Then said these men, We shall not find any occasion against this Daniel, except we find it against him concerning the law of his God. Then these presidents and princes assembled together to the king, and said thus unto him, King Darius, live for ever. All the presidents of the kingdom, the governors, and the princes, the counsellers, and the captains, have consulted together to establish a royal statute, and to make a firm decree, that whosoever shall ask a petition of any God or man for thirty days, save of thee, O king, he shall be cast into the den of lions. Now, O king, establish the decree, and sign the writing, that it be not changed, according to the law of the Medes and Persians, which altereth not. Wherefore king Darius signed the writing and the decree. Now when Daniel knew that the writing was signed, he went into his house; and his windows being open in his chamber toward Jerusalem, he kneeled upon his knees three times a day, and prayed, and gave thanks before his God, as he did aforetime. Then these men assembled, and found Daniel praying and making supplication before his God. Then they came near, and spake before the king concerning the king's decree; Hast thou not signed a decree, that every man that shall ask a petition of any God or man within thirty days, save of thee, O king, shall be cast into the den of lions? The king answered and said, The thing is true, according to the law of the Medes and Persians, which altereth not. Then answered they and said before the king, That Daniel, which is of the children of the captivity of Judah, regardeth not thee, O king, nor the decree that thou hast signed, but maketh his petition three times a day. Then the king, when he heard these words, was sore displeased with himself, and set his heart on Daniel to deliver him: and he laboured till the going down of the sun to deliver him. Then these men assembled unto the king, and said unto the king, Know, O king, that the law of the Medes and Persians is, That no decree nor statute which the king establisheth may be changed. Then the king commanded, and they brought Daniel, and cast him into the den of lions. Now the king spake and said unto Daniel, Thy God whom thou servest continually, he will deliver thee. And a stone was brought, and laid upon the mouth of the den; and the king sealed it with his own signet, and with the signet of his lords; that the purpose might not be changed concerning Daniel. Then the king went to his palace, and passed the night fasting: neither were instruments of musick brought before him: and his sleep went from him. Then the king arose very early in the morning, and went in haste unto the den of lions. And when he came to the den, he cried with a lamentable voice unto Daniel: and the king spake and said to Daniel, O Daniel, servant of the living God, is thy God, whom thou servest continually, able to deliver thee from the lions? Then said Daniel unto the king, O king, live for ever. My God hath sent his angel, and hath shut the lions' mouths, that they have not hurt me: forasmuch as before him innocency was found in me; and also before thee, O king, have I done no hurt. Then was the king exceeding glad for him, and commanded that they should take Daniel up out of the den. So Daniel was taken up out of the den, and no manner of hurt was found upon him, because he believed in his God. And the king commanded, and they brought those men which had accused Daniel, and they cast them into the den of lions, them, their children, and their wives; and the lions had the mastery of them, and brake all their bones in pieces or ever they came at the bottom of the den. Then king Darius wrote unto all people, nations, and languages, that dwell in all the earth; Peace be multiplied unto you. I make a decree, That in every dominion of my kingdom men tremble and fear before the God of Daniel: for he is the living God, and stedfast for ever, and his kingdom that which shall not be destroyed, and his dominion shall be even unto the end. He delivereth and rescueth, and he worketh signs and wonders in heaven and in earth, who hath delivered Daniel from the power of the lions. So this Daniel prospered in the reign of Darius, and in the reign of Cyrus the Persian." (Daniel 6).

Daniel in the Lions' Den

— "Be sober, be vigilant; because your adversary the devil, as a
roaring lion, walketh about, seeking whom he may devour:" —

1 Peter 5:8

Though systems of governance or systems of conquest
May conspire and manifest!
Controlling the populace and oppress
Some autocratic, some democratic, some monarchies, I must confess
That Daniel's God power and authority is simply the best!
A God who is able to deliver in any situation
When enemies seek to bring you down – in a total calculation –
Or conspire a Barabbas – over JESUS of the crucifixion!
When God's Word is used against His daughters and against His
sons
Knoweth today your friends; know your associations!
Or be cast into your own Lions' den
As you pray and honor God's law, as God's children!
You can be cast into the Lions' den or face certain death
Where men of no moral courage may glory yet
But when God is for you, Daniel's God and Savior removes the

threat!
Even though a stone laid and covers the mouth of your den
Remember this day when God rescues from your Lions' den – of
devils and men!
And death, and death, and death!
For 'tis Jehovah who supplies every last breath!

Darius the new king over Babylon, of the Medes and Persians,
thought it best
To set up a system of governance after their conquest
He chose 122 princes
To help in governing the Province
Then over those princes, he chose three presidents and gave
dominion
Above those three presidents, he chose Daniel: a man of esteem and
wisdom
All for the protective quest of the king
So that the princes might give accounts of everything
And the king would suffer no damage of authority
A strategic governing entity of the Medes and Persian society
Daniel, though, was preferred above the princes and presidents for
he had an excellent spirit and attitude
So, the king sought to set him above the whole realm he chose
Envy stepped in – for the presidents and princes sought to discredit
him
They tried everything they knew but couldn't find any fault to win
Then concluded: the only fault they could find against him
concerned the worship of the law of his God!

The conspiracy was set, and they approached the king
Doubling down to get rid of Daniel. They were really conniving

They declared: King Darius, live forever
Live and reign, ever and ever
Declaring still to the king, that all the presidents and all the princes,
the governors, the counselors, and the captains, together consulted
That you, oh king, should be exalted!
Establish now a royal statute, make a firm decree
That whosoever shall make a petition of any God or man for thirty
days – except to thee
Shall be cast into the lions' den
Now, know your associations and know your friend!
In the quest for control, for leadership,
Presidents, princes, and many more conspired and tricked in a quest
for worship
Oh, king, establish and sign the decree that it should not be changed
For actions speak louder; the written words constrained
According to the law of the Medes and the Persians which altereth
not
Sign your name on every dot – every dot!
Every man has a price; any man without principle can be bought!

When Daniel knew that the decree was signed
He knew that it was specially designed
He knew the enemy, the adversary, the roaring lion, conspired to
malign
Yet he went into his house and kneeled; he openly prayed
Three times a day – he openly prayed!
With windows open towards Jerusalem, he prayed and thank God
Great God! He prayed, praise, and honor you – isn't that true faith
in the Lord?
Then those men rallied together and found Daniel in fervent prayer,
petitioning his God,

And informed the king, reminded him about the decree he signed.
For thirty days, all petitioning to any other God or man were outlawed
For anyone found will be cast into the lions' den
Daniel regardeth not thee nor honor your decree. He maketh petition to his God three times a day, without pretend
The King answered and said, "according to the law of the Medes and Persians, the thing is true". Daniel stands condemned
But the King was displeased with himself to be tricked and set his heart to deliver Daniel
He tried everything in his power, exhausting every channel!
Then those men rallied and assembled again before the King
Remember the law of the Medes and Persians, stand supreme over everything
No decree or statute that the king established can be changed
No part of it can be rearranged
So, the King commanded and they brought Daniel
And the King in faith declared: Daniel, your God whom you serve continually, will deliver
But Daniel was cast into the lions' den by the state's law and order
A stone was brought and laid upon the mouth of the den
The king sealed it with his signet and then,
With the signet of his lords, in the presence of all of them
He hurried to the palace in fasting. No music was played and his sleep went from him
His mood was dark and dim
But he arose very early and rushed to the lions' den
And as he came to the den, he cried out aloud, in a lamentable voice!
Daniel, oh Daniel, servant of the living God – this wasn't my doing and my choice

Did your God whom you serve continually deliver you from the
lions?
Daniel answered and said, "Oh, king, live forever; my hope rests in
the God of Zion!"
For God sent his angel and shut the mouths of the lions
For before God, and before thee, my innocence shines like a
diamond!

The King was exceedingly glad
He commanded Daniel be taken from the den. His accusers were
worried and sad!
'Cause he believed in God, no hurt was found on Daniel
But all around the world that day, it was a big, big scandal
The King commanded they brought those men who accused Daniel
– cast them into the lions' den
Also, their children and their wives – cast them into the lions' den
The lions broke their bones to pieces upon the den's floor
Not one was able to escape through the den's shuttered door
Then the King once again penned a new decree!
Herein, we shall see,
Unto all people, nations, languages – unto every part of the
kingdom – men should tremble and fear Daniel's God
He is the living God – steadfast unto the end – and He alone to be
awed
He delivers, performing signs and wonders in the heavens and the
Earth. Get in His favor
So, Daniel prospered in the reign of Darius and in the reign of
Cyrus of Medo-Persia
For Daniel's deliverer is God and Savior!

End.

Reflections

In this well-known story of Danel in the lion's den, we come upon this epic poem of immense proportion. There are two heroes herein, Daniel and King Darius. The poem finds the impeccable work ethics of an individual infused by the Holy Spirit, being envied, bringing about the changing of laws for personal vendetta. We find the demonic spirit of envy, fault finding, conspiracy, and the changing of laws for personal gain; and not for the good of a nation. The imagery must not escape us, as this is the prophecy of the time of the end when laws will be made against God's chosen people. Therefore, the word here is "lion", or the phrase "lion's den". It brings to mind an angry, hungry lion, the Devil, who seeks to do us harm in his den of death. We can juxtapose the literal den of lions in parallel with the devil as a hungry lion. There is more to appreciate about this poem, like the heartless conspirators, the kingdom of peoples (witnesses), and the final judgment. The lions' mouths were literally shut by the angel, with Daniel in the den, whilst Daniel rested peacefully in the face of the lions. This is a testament to God's saving grace. In contrast, King Darius tossed and turned all night long; disturbed until Daniel was extracted safely from the den of ravenous lions.

It is important to interject that when something unfortunate happens to a person, others emotionally connected are also affected. Although Daniel was left unharmed, the next morning his enemies who conspired against him, suffered a worse fate as they were tossed into the den, and snatched up by the ravenous lions. Remember, "weeping may endure for a night, but joy cometh in the morning." (Psalm 30:5) The traits within human beings of a lion are connected to what one hungers for; appealing to the ego, his emotions if left unchecked could destroy him. Later in the poem, King Darius shifts his use of his power to command the people of his kingdom to worship Daniel's God. This is proof that God rules governments, and change is possible, "For kingship belongs to the Lord, and He rules over the nations" (Psalm 22:28). The challenge is to pray without ceasing while at home, work, and recreation, to the one who keeps us balanced in our emotions (ego) until change comes. If there is a group of people or individuals conspiring against you; ignore them, fast, and pray to God about the matter; trust in His sure deliverance and God will set you free. My challenge to you is to continue to peruse these poetic lines that point you only to God.

Chapter 6 Prayer

Dear God, forgive me and save me from my lion's den of life's dangers. I will stand for you by your grace and mercy towards me. Please remove the threats and close the mouths of the lions that seek to do me harm. Stop them in their tracks who seek to devour me! My prayer is for deliverance today. In Jesus' name. Amen.

Personal Reflections

Daniel 7

"In the first year of Belshazzar king of Babylon Daniel had a dream and visions of his head upon his bed: then he wrote the dream, and told the sum of the matters. Daniel spake and said, I saw in my vision by night, and, behold, the four winds of the heaven strove upon the great sea. And four great beasts came up from the sea, diverse one from another. The first was like a lion, and had eagle's wings: I beheld till the wings thereof were plucked, and it was lifted up from the earth, and made stand upon the feet as a man, and a man's heart was given to it. And behold another beast, a second, like to a bear, and it raised up itself on one side, and it had three ribs in the mouth of it between the teeth of it: and they said thus unto it, Arise, devour much flesh. After this I beheld, and lo another, like a leopard, which had upon the back of it four wings of a fowl; the beast had also four heads; and dominion was given to it. After this I saw in the night visions, and behold a fourth beast, dreadful and terrible, and strong exceedingly; and it had great iron teeth: it devoured and brake in pieces, and stamped the residue with the feet of it: and it was diverse from all the beasts that were before it; and it had ten horns. I considered the horns, and, behold, there came up among them another little horn, before whom there were three of the first horns plucked up by the roots: and, behold, in this horn were eyes like the eyes of man, and a mouth speaking great things. I beheld till the thrones were cast down, and the Ancient of days did sit, whose garment was white as snow, and the hair of his head like the pure wool: his throne was like the fiery flame, and his wheels as burning fire. A fiery stream issued and came forth from before him: thousand thousands ministered unto him, and ten thousand times ten thousand stood before him: the judgment was set, and the books were opened. I beheld then because of the voice of the great words which the horn spake: I beheld even till the beast was slain, and his body destroyed, and given to the burning flame. As concerning the rest of the beasts, they had their dominion taken away: yet their lives were prolonged for a season and time. I saw in the night visions, and, behold, one like the Son of man came with the clouds of heaven, and came to the Ancient of days, and they brought him near before him. And there was given him dominion, and glory, and a kingdom, that all people, nations, and languages, should serve him: his dominion is an everlasting dominion, which shall not pass away, and his kingdom that which shall not be destroyed. I Daniel was grieved in my spirit in the midst of my body, and the visions of my head troubled me. I came near unto one of them that stood by, and asked him the truth of all this. So he told me, and made me know the interpretation of the things. These great beasts, which are four, are four kings, which shall arise out of the earth. But the saints of the most High shall take the kingdom, and possess the kingdom for ever, even for ever and ever. Then I would know the truth of the fourth beast, which was diverse from all the others, exceeding dreadful, whose teeth were of iron, and his nails of brass; which devoured, brake in pieces, and stamped the residue with his feet; And of the ten horns that were in his head, and of the other which came up, and before whom three fell; even of that horn that had eyes, and a mouth that spake very great things, whose look was more stout than his fellows. I beheld, and the same horn made war with the saints, and prevailed against them; Until the Ancient of days came, and judgment was given to the saints of the most High; and the time came that the saints possessed the kingdom. Thus he said, The fourth beast shall be the fourth kingdom upon earth, which shall be diverse from all kingdoms, and shall devour the whole earth, and shall tread it down, and break it in pieces. And the ten horns out of this kingdom are ten kings that shall arise: and another shall rise after them; and he shall be diverse from the first, and he shall subdue three kings. And he shall speak great words against the most High, and shall wear out the saints of the most High, and think to change times and laws: and they shall be given into his hand until a time and times and the dividing of time. But the judgment shall sit, and they shall take away his dominion, to consume and to destroy it unto the end. And the kingdom and dominion, and the greatness of the kingdom under the whole heaven, shall be given to the people of the saints of the most High, whose kingdom is an everlasting kingdom, and all dominions shall serve and obey him. Hitherto is the end of the matter. As for me Daniel, my cogitations much troubled me, and my countenance changed in me: but I kept the matter in my heart." (Daniel 7).

In the Vision of Daniel: Beasts, Winds, and Wings

— "For I know the thoughts I think toward you, saith the Lord, thoughts of peace, not of evil, to give you an expected end"
—Jeremiah 29:11

On this glorious day of deliverance
God will remove wrongs and ignorance!
Gift again by His sacred name, the reward of everlasting life (Daniel 7:9-14; 7:18; 7:22; 7:26,27)
The saints shall judge all, bringing an end to the long-lasting strife!
Whilst the Ancient of Days, God is He, sits on the heavenly throne
When God is for you – for me and you – you're never ever alone!
He rides and flies on cherubs' wings, commanding angels, in protection true
For God is an energetic lover of man – if you only knew!
With power, with glory, transported throughout the galaxy and skies
God's love truly, truly mystifies!

In the vision of Daniel
There came up four beasts empaneled

It happened in the days of King Belshazzar
The son of Nabonidus, grandson of King Nebuchadnezzar
Winds roared upon the great sea
The Lion with Eagle's Wings, I did see
Plucked wings, standing like a lion-hearted man
These are things, we need to understand.

Then appeared a bear, predictively
With three ribs clutched in his mouth, and stand
With an upraised side
Ready to devour the land, terribly.

The Leopard came, sporting wings of a fowl to fly
Complementarily with four heads and dominion at its command.

The fourth beast, though – dreadful, terrible, and strong
Devouring and breaking, stamping down those before, with teeth of
iron
Spouting ten horns!
Then the upstarted little horn, pluck three
Proud! Like destiny!
Displaying eyes and mouth of a man
What is there not to understand?

What a dangerous time to live this mystery
Religion and State cementing: conniving: prosecuting
With crushing hate
Even the elect, God must consecrate.

Judgment now set
With the Ancient of Days
As glory surround Him, The Lion of Zion soon cometh

With chariots of clouds.
The Son escorted – at the crowning met
All kingdoms, and nations, and peoples, and languages to serve Him
Come confess, He's King of kings yet.

Though four Kings came, and the little horn arose
Desiring worship
But had their dominion reproved
And forfeit.

With tenacity and trickery
That little horn made war with the saints
That's the papacy!
But true love, can't be constrained
For this is the story of the Lamb's destiny.

He is the Son of Man!
King of kings, Lord of lords!
Coming on the clouds of glory!
With Power: with Glory: and Dominion.

To see God as He is
Look to the Savior He supplies and gives
For only one Savior died: yet the Son of Man lives
God used the four empaneled beasts
The Lion: The Bear: The Leopard: The Dreadful, Terrible and
Strong Beast: false worship: and false priests
Just to tell of the battle of Satan's lust for control and power
His destruction is sure: of the day and the hour.

Confused yourself not with the differing faiths
Immersed in God's love: washed by His shed blood: He consecrates

It's a mystery: yet a mystery revealed!
God is not a deluded old man who can't feel
He is not made of stone: or inanimate things
When you're lonely: fearful and unhappy: God's heart pains and
rings and rings and rings.

End.

Reflections

The Ancient of Days (God) has finally stepped into our panoramic vision in Daniel chapter 7, in all of His glory. However, this poem brings alive the ferocious nature of Satan, with an artful depiction of the four ferocious beasts. Within the interpretation of the vision, we discover the characteristics of an earthly state (Rome) carrying out Satan's hatred towards all believers (not divided groups by religious affiliation) of Jesus Christ. The poet describes the Ancient of Days and the Lion of Zion's characteristics as triumphant against the earthly powerful kingdoms. Therefore, the challenge in today's world is to remain faithful and persevere through the terrible time of trouble as never was before a nation. The words or phrase "Ancient of Days" can only apply to God Almighty (Daniel 7:9). It is God in all His glory as judge! Look again and again at this poetic masterpiece to find how God's love mystifies. Thank God that at the end of earth's history, the elect of God will be triumphant against all persecution.

Chapter 7 Prayer

Loving Lord, thank you for your mystifying love towards us. Even though we do not deserve it, forgive us and prepare us for your glorious appearance. We will celebrate; for the lion, the bear, the leopard, the dreadful terrible and strong beast, false worship, and false priests will all be gone! For only one Savior died and rose again, and will come in the clouds with glory; then we will sing redemption songs and tell our story. Thank you for such a Savior! In Jesus' sweet and matchless name. Amen.

Personal Reflections

_____

_____

_____

_____

_____

_____

_____

_____

_____

Daniel 8

"In the third year of the reign of king Belshazzar a vision appeared unto me, even unto me Daniel, after that which appeared unto me at the first. And I saw in a vision; and it came to pass, when I saw, that I was at Shushan in the palace, which is in the province of Elam; and I saw in a vision, and I was by the river of Ulai. Then I lifted up mine eyes, and saw, and, behold, there stood before the river a ram which had two horns: and the two horns were high; but one was higher than the other, and the higher came up last. I saw the ram pushing westward, and northward, and southward; so that no beasts might stand before him, neither was there any that could deliver out of his hand; but he did according to his will, and became great. And as I was considering, behold, an he goat came from the west on the face of the whole earth, and touched not the ground: and the goat had a notable horn between his eyes. And he came to the ram that had two horns, which I had seen standing before the river, and ran unto him in the fury of his power. And I saw him come close unto the ram, and he was moved with choler against him, and smote the ram, and brake his two horns: and there was no power in the ram to stand before him, but he cast him down to the ground, and stamped upon him: and there was none that could deliver the ram out of his hand. Therefore the he goat waxed very great: and when he was strong, the great horn was broken; and for it came up four notable ones toward the four winds of heaven. And out of one of them came forth a little horn, which waxed exceeding great, toward the south, and toward the east, and toward the pleasant land. And it waxed great, even to the host of heaven; and it cast down some of the host and of the stars to the ground, and stamped upon them. Yea, he magnified himself even to the prince of the host, and by him the daily sacrifice was taken away, and the place of his sanctuary was cast down. And an host was given him against the daily sacrifice by reason of transgression, and it cast down the truth to the ground; and it practised, and prospered. Then I heard one saint speaking, and another saint said unto that certain saint which spake, How long shall be the vision concerning the daily sacrifice, and the transgression of desolation, to give both the sanctuary and the host to be trodden under foot? And he said unto me, Unto two thousand and three hundred days; then shall the sanctuary be cleansed. And it came to pass, when I, even I Daniel, had seen the vision, and sought for the meaning, then, behold, there stood before me as the appearance of a man. And I heard a man's voice between the banks of Ulai, which called, and said, Gabriel, make this man to understand the vision. So he came near where I stood: and when he came, I was afraid, and fell upon my face: but he said unto me, Understand, O son of man: for at the time of the end shall be the vision. Now as he was speaking with me, I was in a deep sleep on my face toward the ground: but he touched me, and set me upright. And he said, Behold, I will make thee know what shall be in the last end of the indignation: for at the time appointed the end shall be. The ram which thou sawest having two horns are the kings of Media and Persia. And the rough goat is the king of Grecia: and the great horn that is between his eyes is the first king. Now that being broken, whereas four stood up for it, four kingdoms shall stand up out of the nation, but not in his power. And in the latter time of their kingdom, when the transgressors are come to the full, a king of fierce countenance, and understanding dark sentences, shall stand up. And his power shall be mighty, but not by his own power: and he shall destroy wonderfully, and shall prosper, and practise, and shall destroy the mighty and the holy people. And through his policy also he shall cause craft to prosper in his hand; and he shall magnify himself in his heart, and by peace shall destroy many: he shall also stand up against the Prince of princes; but he shall be broken without hand. And the vision of the evening and the morning which was told is true: wherefore shut thou up the vision; for it shall be for many days. And I Daniel fainted, and was sick certain days; afterward I rose up, and did the king's business; and I was astonished at the vision, but none understood it." (Daniel 8).

Amazing Vision

— The Ram Empowered, The He-Goat of Wrath, The Little Horn Magnified —

— "Humble yourselves in the sight of the Lord, and he shall lift you up" — (James 4:10)

The chapter and book are clear
Evidential: essential: prophetical and dear!
Drawing all nearer to the Master and Lord
As High Priest: as Creator and God!
For no kingdom: both great and small
Can stop God's judgment: and atonement for all!
Medo- Persia, Greece, or the king of bold countenance with power great
Ever will stand eternally damned: that shall be their fate!
For Christ: our compassionate High Priest who died: lives for our salvation (Hebrews 3:1; 8:12)
The little horn that trampled the sanctuary: Christ defeats: in the story of redemption!
Catch the vision: it's time for the Great Commission
Gathering all: from across the world: this is the mission!

153

For when connected to His word
No weapon formed against us: can harm us: the devil trembles at the
name of our God!
As the remnant: nothing can confuse: nor deceive us
For our Savior: His name is Jesus!
The symbolic Tamid saves: In the continual ministry of Christ
Our High Priest: our soon coming King: the living, living, loving
sacrifice!

In the third year of King Belshazzar, I saw another amazing vision
It appeared to be in Shushan, the capital city of the province of Elam
Locked in the vicinity of the river Ulai
Fully present, I raised my eyes
And saw a ram, standing at the bank of the river
With two horns, both horns high, but one higher than the other
The higher horn came up last
It came up sneakily and fast
The ram charging westward, northward, and southward
No beast or no one could stand or rescue: the ram was empowered!
He magnified himself and did as he pleased
For wanton power cannot be appeased!

As I was taking stock of the situation
A he-goat came from the west without touching the ground
Across the whole earth in prolific animation
With a conspicuous horn between his eyes
He came to the ram with the two horns standing at the river Ulai
He ran and flew, enraged in a mighty wrath
It's time to count and do the math
He struck the ram and broke his two horns
Cast him down to the ground, trampled upon him in utter scorn

No one could rescue the ram from its power
Then the he-goat magnified himself exceedingly from that hour
Although he was strong, the great horn then broke
And in its stead, came up four conspicuous horns in a masterstroke
Glaringly towards the four winds of heaven or the power of God
It's time to call on the King of kings, and Lord of lords
For out of them came forth a little horn
Hungry for worship; many will die, and many will burn
The little horn grew exceedingly great toward the south, toward the
east, and toward the pleasant land (Deuteronomy 26:3, Acts
15:16-17)
Even toward the host of heaven, casting some of the hosts of the
stars upon the ground: What is there not to understand?
The little horn magnified itself, even to the Prince of the host
(Joshua 5:14, 25; 10:21; 21:1)
With a puffed-up chest and a mouth that boast
The continual burnt offering was taken away
The place of the sanctuary was overthrown that day (AD 70)
And the host was given over to the little horn
The man of sin, the son of perdition and scorn (2 Thessalonians
2:3-4)
The little horn of Daniel eight parallels and increases
Of the little horn of Daniel seven, and the beasts
For in Daniel two and seven, Rome follows Greece
Also, in Daniel eight, Rome arose in the west, out of one of the
"four winds"
For Pagan and Christian Rome like a continuum of sins
Roman bishop as the successor to the Roman emperor
Hear the whispering sound of a worshiper
Telling of the crucified Jesus and the Father

155

For Jesus is the true fulfillment, intercessor, and Savior
The little horn is a symbol of a kingdom
Like the sanctuary is a symbol that cannot be restricted: Get wisdom
In Daniel two and seven, metals and animals are symbols for
successive empires
The cleansing of the sanctuary is broader and richer, like a fire that
inspires (Daniel 8:13-14)
For when the little horn magnified
Oh, Lord! Dear Lord, with me, abide!
Remember: Jesus is the true High Priest of our confession (Hebrews
3:1, 8:1-2)
Though the continual burnt offering, take away all transgression
When truth was cast down to the ground
The little horn acted, and prospered, even with aggression!
Then I heard a holy one speaking
Another holy one said to the one that spoke and weeping
"For how long the vision is concerning the continual burnt offering
"The transgression that makes desolate
"And the giving over of the sanctuary and the host to be trampled
underfoot?"
Trying to understand, couldn't understand, misunderstood
What does Daniel eight verse fourteen (Daniel 8:14) symbolizes
Only a few realize
"For two thousand and three hundred evenings and mornings; then
the sanctuary shall be restored to its rightful state" (Genesis 1:5,6;
Ezekiel 4:6)
I really need God to strengthen my faith
Still troubling my heart though
Everyone should know
The prophecy of Daniel eight verse fourteen (Daniel 8:14)

"Unto two thousand and three hundred days; then shall the
sanctuary be cleansed," what does it really mean? (Genesis 1:5,6;
Ezekiel 4:6)
Awaiting still the explanation from angel Gabriel
It's more than territorial
For the man's voice between the banks of the River Ulai ordered
"Gabriel, make this man understand the vision," must be the Son of
Man who conquered (Mark 14:62; John 3:13; Daniel 7:13-14; Luke
5:24)
In fright, I fell on my face as Gabriel appeared
This is the fact, not a simple scare
Then Gabriel said, "Understand, son of man," have no fear
"The vision is for the time of the end" you comprehend?
As he spoke, I fell into a deep sleep with face to the ground
He touches me, placed my feet on solid ground, he turns me around
Then declared, I will make known the indignation
For it will be the appointed time of the end of judgment
(Atonement) for all nations!

The ram with the two horns at the bank of the River Ulai
These are the kings of Media and Persia; I tell you no lie
The he-goat is the King of Greece
Must be Alexander the Great, the military strategist
For the great horn between the eyes is the first king
Then the horn was broken, and four arose
The generals: Cassander, Ptolemy, Antigonus, and Seleucus:
juxtaposed
Now to expose at the end of their rule
Out from the carnage of the transgressors' misrule
A king with a bold countenance who understands riddles shall arise
His power shall be great: succeeding in what he does: while the

saints will cry

His cunning shall make deceit prosper

As he magnifies himself against the Prince of princes: a fake and an
impostor

Not by human hand can he be broken

This vision of the evenings and the mornings is true: but seal up the
vision: God has spoken

This vision is not to be fulfilled in Daniel's day

Daniel was overcome, in his sickbed he lay

He was appalled by the vision

But it was appointed for the time of the end!

End.

Reflections

In this vision, this poetic work exemplifies that there was a transition from the power of the Medes and Persians to Greece, followed by the little horn power of Rome, down to the ages of time. As the poet declares, within it lies evidential, essential, and prophetical information that points us to the atoning ministry of Christ in the heavenly sanctuary. We find in this poem the rhythm of call and response, praise and chastisement, and the endless bounty of forgiveness resident in God. It is a poetic expression like a psalm or song, in total demonstration and support of the Great Commission. Think about the allusion to contemporary history that mirrors this narrative expressed in these lines to appreciate it. Sometimes the face of beauty, or poetry, or even of truth is not apparent. However, look again at the expression of the narrative. Is this what you expected or even wanted to hear? The word here is "evidential". It is based on evidence and the supporting evidence is given as clear as day in graphic detail. The structure or form is sociohistorical, written in a quest to be truthful, practical, and logical. Go beyond the obvious: look at our times, into the minutiae lives we live. Look around you, in your community, your church, your school, your club, your peers, your family to see the truth herein and the beauty in the poetry and the truth foretold.

Chapter 8 Prayer

Heavenly Father, let us not be dismayed by the wanton power some display. Nor worry about the things that are coming upon the face of the Earth. For you are our God and will deliver us. Let us tune in to you and draw us closer to our Lord and Master. Forgive us and empower us to the Great Commission of your word. Therefore, let us mystify the world with the message of your grace. In this cause, we seek your protection, help to live right and empowerment of your Holy Spirit. Then, no weapon formed against us will prosper. Thank you, Lord, for hearing and for answering. In Jesus' name. Amen.

Personal Reflections

_____

_____

_____

_____

_____

_____

_____

_____

_____

Daniel 9

"In the first year of Darius the son of Ahasuerus, of the seed of the Medes, which was made king over the realm of the Chaldeans; In the first year of his reign I Daniel understood by books the number of the years, whereof the word of the Lord came to Jeremiah the prophet, that he would accomplish seventy years in the desolations of Jerusalem. And I set my face unto the Lord God, to seek by prayer and supplications, with fasting, and sackcloth, and ashes: And I prayed unto the Lord my God, and made my confession, and said, O Lord, the great and dreadful God, keeping the covenant and mercy to them that love him, and to them that keep his commandments; We have sinned, and have committed iniquity, and have done wickedly, and have rebelled, even by departing from thy precepts and from thy judgments: Neither have we hearkened unto thy servants the prophets, which spake in thy name to our kings, our princes, and our fathers, and to all the people of the land. O Lord, righteousness belongeth unto thee, but unto us confusion of faces, as at this day; to the men of Judah, and to the inhabitants of Jerusalem, and unto all Israel, that are near, and that are far off, through all the countries whither thou hast driven them, because of their trespass that they have trespassed against thee. O Lord, to us belongeth confusion of face, to our kings, to our princes, and to our fathers, because we have sinned against thee. To the Lord our God belong mercies and forgivenesses, though we have rebelled against him; Neither have we obeyed the voice of the Lord our God, to walk in his laws, which he set before us by his servants the prophets. Yea, all Israel have transgressed thy law, even by departing, that they might not obey thy voice; therefore the curse is poured upon us, and the oath that is written in the law of Moses the servant of God, because we have sinned against him. And he hath confirmed his words, which he spake against us, and against our judges that judged us, by bringing upon us a great evil: for under the whole heaven hath not been done as hath been done upon Jerusalem. As it is written in the law of Moses, all this evil is come upon us: yet made we not our prayer before the Lord our God, that we might turn from our iniquities, and understand thy truth. Therefore hath the Lord watched upon the evil, and brought it upon us: for the Lord our God is righteous in all his works which he doeth: for we obeyed not his voice. And now, O Lord our God, that hast brought thy people forth out of the land of Egypt with a mighty hand, and hast gotten thee renown, as at this day; we have sinned, we have done wickedly. O Lord, according to all thy righteousness, I beseech thee, let thine anger and thy fury be turned away from thy city Jerusalem, thy holy mountain: because for our sins, and for the iniquities of our fathers, Jerusalem and thy people are become a reproach to all that are about us. Now therefore, O our God, hear the prayer of thy servant, and his supplications, and cause thy face to shine upon thy sanctuary that is desolate, for the Lord's sake. O my God, incline thine ear, and hear; open thine eyes, and behold our desolations, and the city which is called by thy name: for we do not present our supplications before thee for our righteousnesses, but for thy great mercies. O Lord, hear; O Lord, forgive; O Lord, hearken and do; defer not, for thine own sake, O my God: for thy city and thy people are called by thy name. And whiles I was speaking, and praying, and confessing my sin and the sin of my people Israel, and presenting my supplication before the Lord my God for the holy mountain of my God; Yea, whiles I was speaking in prayer, even the man Gabriel, whom I had seen in the vision at the beginning, being caused to fly swiftly, touched me about the time of the evening oblation. And he informed me, and talked with me, and said, O Daniel, I am now come forth to give thee skill and understanding. At the beginning of thy supplications the commandment came forth, and I am come to shew thee; for thou art greatly beloved: therefore understand the matter, and consider the vision. Seventy weeks are determined upon thy people and upon thy holy city, to finish the transgression, and to make an end of sins, and to make reconciliation for iniquity, and to bring in everlasting righteousness, and to seal up the vision and prophecy, and to anoint the most Holy. Know therefore and understand, that from the going forth of the commandment to restore and to build Jerusalem unto the Messiah the Prince shall be seven weeks, and threescore and two weeks: the street shall be built again, and the wall, even in troublous times. And after threescore and two weeks shall Messiah be cut off, but not for himself: and the people of the prince that shall come shall destroy the city and the sanctuary; and the end thereof shall be with a flood, and unto the end of the war desolations are determined. And he shall confirm the covenant with many for one week: and in the midst of the week he shall cause the sacrifice and the oblation to cease, and for the overspreading of abominations he shall make it desolate, even until the consummation, and that determined shall be poured upon the desolate." (Daniel 9).

Daniel's Power-Packed Prayer: Israel's Intercessor

— God Will Make Everything Absolutely All Right —

— "For God so love the world, that he gave his only begotten son, that whosoever believeth in him, should not perish but have everlasting life" — John 3:16

This is the story: about the cleansing: of the heavenly sanctuary
Prayer moves mountains: strength comes from testaments old and new: God's Library!
Watering the mind: in righteousness: from His word
Claiming the promises: seeking the glory of God (Jeremiah 29:13)
Holy Spirit: channel my words: don't return them void: amazed enemies destroyed
In total communication: prayer flies
Uniting in His sanctuary: calling His name: His blood cries
Once dead: touched by His blood: am alive
In my sinfulness: composing my prayer
Standing on the promises of Christ: to deliver
Clamoring for mercy: not in the vestibule of the earthly
Now: Christ dwells in the heavenly sanctuary

And: only the Son of Man: can save
From the uttermost: to the grave
He is the resurrection and life: who reigns in glory
Telling of the redemption story: of Christ who dwells in majesty! In majesty!

The year that Darius sat as vassal King on the throne
After Babylon was overthrown
Ushering in the silver kingdom of Medo-Persia
Daniel checked the books and the writings of Jeremiah
How much longer for the desolation of the Temple, and Jerusalem's destiny
Optimistic, yet fearful, concerned extremely
Might not the seventy-year prophecy about to end?
Must alert the nation of Jewish children!
Must consecrate ourselves
The prophecy of Jeremiah compels (Jer 29:10-14)
Let me kiss the streets of Jerusalem rebuilt, and dwell
Amidst the magnificence of Israel!

Daniel prayed in sackcloth and ashes
Fasting, supplicating, his tears flashes
Praying and confessing for himself and the Jewish masses
Oh! Great and dreadful God, remember your covenant
Though our sins cascading and predominant
Remember our love as a Commandment keeping people
Immersed in sin, but you're our example
We ignored your prophets, who spoke in your name
Ignored your precepts and your judgments again and again
We have done wickedly
But lift the clouds! restore our blessings, our destiny

Let your face shine o'er the city

Forgive our kings, forgive our princes, forgive our forefathers

Forgive me, my sisters, my brothers

We have transgressed your law

We did not hold you and your prophets in awe

You are God: Our Lord: Our Father

Of all of Judah, of Jerusalem, and all of Israel

Grateful your judgment is impartial

With memories trending: Brought us out of Egypt, with a mighty hand

Come turn away your fury from Jerusalem:

Your holy mountain: God, please understand

Hear the prayer of your servant: Hear our desolation

You are God of Creation: God of every Nation

Grant to us full restoration

You have now punished Babylon

With the Medes and Persians

Restore the apple of thy eye

The tears we cry!!! The tears we cry!!!

Righteousness alone belongs to you

Praying your blessings for each morning renewed

Calm the storm of life

Dry the sea of despair and strife

Great God! deliver from the distresses

Your blessings come expresses

Come in the midst of prayer

Fly Angel Gabriel with wings of thunder

To deliver! To deliver! To deliver!

Thank you, Lord: Thank you, Father

Living in Daniel's power-packed prayer!

Daniel, now concerned with the calculation of time
It's not infinite but definite and prophetically designed
Seventy weeks are determined
To finish the transgressions
To make an end of sin
To make reconciliation for iniquity
These three repeated statements
All kinds of sins finished and seal off by atonement (Lev 16:21)
To seal up the vision and prophecy
To bring in everlasting righteousness
And to anoint the most holy!
Here comes Christ, bringing everlasting righteousness (Hebrews
9:11-26)
From the foundation of time to all who're impressed
For the answer is more than Daniel was praying
It depicts the holy city New Jerusalem (Revelation 21:2)
This is what Gabriel was trying to explain
Time to be discerning! Time to be discerning!
Could be extremely complicating
Or conflicting, or conflicting
The angel Gabriel specially commissioned, explaining
Trisecting the Seventy into three segments
Decree to restore and rebuild Jerusalem and government (457 BC)
Remember that the evening and morning is one day (Genesis 1:5,8;
Ezekiel 4:6)
Pray God for the anointing to stay
Rejoice! Rejoice! Rejoice today!
No need for sackcloth, ashes, fasting, and supplication
Get off your knees, time for exulting and praising
Seven weeks equals a forty-nine years content (49 years/ 408BC)

Sixty-two weeks is a four hundred and thirty-four years: extent (434
years/AD34)
One week equals a seven years indent (7 years/AD 34)
Subdividing the final week into halves of three and a half years each,
in an exact dividend (3 1/2 — AD 31, Jesus crucified & AD 27, Jesus
was anointed by the Holy Spirit; dove descended)

Daniel sought a spiritual answer to his prayer
And received a spiritual answer
Daniel asked forgiveness for the Jewish people
Go search the words, don't climb a steeple
God promised forgiveness for everyone, all who assemble
Though Daniel prayed for the restoration of the Jewish temple
God pointed him to the heavenly temple: the heavenly sanctuary
For Jesus would atone and accomplished our destiny
As the ever-living sacrifice on Calvary
Christ Jesus the promised Messiah
Catch the glimpse of the crucified Savior!

End.

Reflections

The humility in this prayer of Daniel comes in the physical demonstration of the sackcloth and ashes. The poetry brings bare the emotions of the moment and dramatizes the pain of it all. There's no pretense but reverence and belief in God's deliverance. It is my hope that genuine prayer and fasting can form a part of our lives to realize our dreams for a Christ-centered life. Appreciate the fact that you can come boldly to the throne of grace in any garb, in any fashion, but only in all reverence with a genuine disposition for deliverance (Hebrews 4:16). Let the beauty of the poetry take you on the journey it weaves, through the despair, fear, and hope. The artistry of the poetry, with words like "vestibule of the earthly" resonates. The etymology of "vestibule" brings us to the idea that in that place one is not ready; not vest (in many ways) not dressed. You need to be taken into the sanctuary presence of God for deliverance. Sackcloth, ashes? What does one wear to approach the Almighty God? From where comes the inner and outer humility? The juxtaposition of inner and outer in the human persona comes into play here. What is real? When will the human recognize his "humanness"? His need to put on the armor of God in and out? The Apostle Paul urges us to, "Put on the whole armor of God, that ye may be able to stand against the wiles of the devil (Ephesians 6:11). We find that Christ is the one who imputes His righteousness to us in saving us. I challenge you to find more beauty and truth in the poetry by looking at it again and again.

Chapter 9 Prayer

Father, I do not dare to limit your awesomeness. Please forgive and let your glory permeates my soul. How much longer must I wait on your deliverance. When will I kiss the streets of Jerusalem renewed and my life imbued with your power? Oh my God hear my cry, hear my plead, forgive my faults and remove everything that is unlike you from me. Secure my God-given destiny. Please visit my limitations and lift me out of my failing situations. Grant to me the victory today. In Jesus' name. Amen.

Personal Reflections

_____

_____

_____

_____

_____

_____

_____

_____

_____

Daniel 10

"In the third year of Cyrus king of Persia a thing was revealed unto Daniel, whose name was called Belteshazzar; and the thing was true, but the time appointed was long: and he understood the thing, and had understanding of the vision. In those days I Daniel was mourning three full weeks. I ate no pleasant bread, neither came flesh nor wine in my mouth, neither did I anoint myself at all, till three whole weeks were fulfilled. And in the four and twentieth day of the first month, as I was by the side of the great river, which is Hiddekel; Then I lifted up mine eyes, and looked, and behold a certain man clothed in linen, whose loins were girded with fine gold of Uphaz: His body also was like the beryl, and his face as the appearance of lightning, and his eyes as lamps of fire, and his arms and his feet like in colour to polished brass, and the voice of his words like the voice of a multitude. And I Daniel alone saw the vision: for the men that were with me saw not the vision; but a great quaking fell upon them, so that they fled to hide themselves. Therefore I was left alone, and saw this great vision, and there remained no strength in me: for my comeliness was turned in me into corruption, and I retained no strength. Yet heard I the voice of his words: and when I heard the voice of his words, then was I in a deep sleep on my face, and my face toward the ground. And, behold, an hand touched me, which set me upon my knees and upon the palms of my hands. And he said unto me, O Daniel, a man greatly beloved, understand the words that I speak unto thee, and stand upright: for unto thee am I now sent. And when he had spoken this word unto me, I stood trembling. Then said he unto me, Fear not, Daniel: for from the first day that thou didst set thine heart to understand, and to chasten thyself before thy God, thy words were heard, and I am come for thy words. But the prince of the kingdom of Persia withstood me one and twenty days: but, lo, Michael, one of the chief princes, came to help me; and I remained there with the kings of Persia. Now I am come to make thee understand what shall befall thy people in the latter days: for yet the vision is for many days. And when he had spoken such words unto me, I set my face toward the ground, and I became dumb. And, behold, one like the similitude of the sons of men touched my lips: then I opened my mouth, and spake, and said unto him that stood before me, O my lord, by the vision my sorrows are turned upon me, and I have retained no strength. For how can the servant of this my lord talk with this my lord? for as for me, straightway there remained no strength in me, neither is there breath left in me. Then there came again and touched me one like the appearance of a man, and he strengthened me, And said, O man greatly beloved, fear not: peace be unto thee, be strong, yea, be strong. And when he had spoken unto me, I was strengthened, and said, Let my lord speak; for thou hast strengthened me. Then said he, Knowest thou wherefore I come unto thee? and now will I return to fight with the prince of Persia: and when I am gone forth, lo, the prince of Grecia shall come. But I will shew thee that which is noted in the scripture of truth: and there is none that holdeth with me in these things, but Michael your prince." (Daniel 10).

Fear Not

— God's Angels/Against The Fallen Angels —

— "Likewise, I say unto you, there is joy in the presence of the angels of God over one sinner that repenteth"— Luke 15:10

Let me tell my revelations: let me read my Daniel's
Telling of the supernatural struggle: of Gabriel: and fallen angels!
Fighting: wrestling to save mankind
The angelic host: so divine!
In this great battle: in military precision
The host of heaven: in war footing: life and death their mission!
Left at my river of Heddekel: finishing in Daniel 12
My heart which never thought to see: my angel: in living color myself!
Beautiful smile: so glorious
Streaking 'cross the living room wall: victorious!
High above the sky: in softest blessedness
In fright: in awe: and in happiness!
O Savior and lord: shouting glory to God
How not to praise the Father: Holy Spirit and Lord!
In tears of joy and gladness

In the pomp of it all: and in the stillness!
In reaching for a poem: or in reaching for a song
God in all His Highness: still condescends: to come along!
The angel of God: appeared to me: whilst writing 12 of Daniel's
Knowing of our struggles: with fallen angels!
Who often: tries to attack
Then, in strength of word and deed, my Savior in reverse smack
attack!
Now in victory: to stand before my God
My Savior: King of kings: and Lord! and Lord!

It was in the third year of Cyrus, King of Persia
When Daniel, called Belteshazzar
Experienced a vision that he understood
The vision was true, though long as it should
'Cause of concern over the opposition: of rebuilding the temple in
Jerusalem
Daniel felt dismayed, empty, and solemn
He was in mourning, fasting, praying: Daniel calling on Israel's
savior
For three weeks: the ultimate prayer warrior!
From the fourth to the twenty-fourth of the first month of the year:
encompassing Passover (Daniel 10:4)
In a singular reminder
Of God's care, deliverance and mighty power (Exodus 12:1-11)
Secluded by the great river Tigris or Hiddekel
Daniel petitioned God for another miracle
Like in Daniel 2, where he gave him the interpretation of the dream
Like in Daniel 6:when God sent an angel to tame the lions: a great
salvific scene
Like in Daniel 9, God sent His highest created angel Gabriel

To Daniel: representative of Yahweh: A God, so Faithful, Majestic,
and Imperial
As he petitioned God at this great river
He lifted up his eyes: only to behold and discover
He beholds a glorious vision of a man
Clothed in linen, with girded loins with fine gold of Uphaz: it's time
to understand
His body like a beryl, a precious stone (Exodus 28:20)
His face the appearance of lightening: fully blown
His arm and feet like polished brass
And the voice of His words like multitudes: commanding, deep and
vast!
At the river Heddekel: Daniel alone saw the vision
And though his companions didn't see it: a quaking fell upon them:
they fled their station: in Olympian fashion.

Left alone in this great vision
All strength was gone: and comeliness was turned into corruption
In deep sleep on his face: Daniel heard the voice of the words to him
Then the hand of the man touched his limb
Placed him on his knees and the palms of his hands
He made no demand: just a command to understand
He said, "O Daniel, a man greatly beloved, understand"
"Understand the words that I speak unto thee, and stand"
Daniel stood trembling
He said, "fear not, Daniel," your heart is set to understand the
meaning
You chastened yourself before your God: I hastened to come
But the prince of Persia withstood me twenty days and one
But Michael came to help me and remained there: Have no fears
Understand what will happen to your people in the latter days

For the vision is yet for many days

As he spoke: Daniel fell on his face and became dumb

Then one like the sons of men touched his lip

Daniel opened his mouth and then he said: lord by the vision my

sorrows overcome: can't catch myself, can't get my grip

There is no strength in me nor no breath

How can the servant of this my lord talk with this my lord: I'm

death

Then one like the appearance of a man: touched him and strength

returned

He then said, "greatly beloved, fear not," be not concerned

Fear not: peace, be strong: be strong

Daniel was strengthened: now to sing an overcomer's song

Let my lord speak: my strength renewed

Then he said, "knowest thou wherefore I come to thee?

Must now return to fight the prince of Persia: but still must let you

see

The prince of Greece will come

Do not worry about it none

I will tell you scriptural truths

For in all of scripture is truth – only Michael your Prince is better:

For He is the Prince of Peace and David's root. (Revelation 22:16;

Isaiah 9:6)

End.

Reflections

We as a people must pay attention to our times, our revelations, circumstances, and utterances. We should allow for something greater than self and petition in all earnestly for clarity. Fortunately, for most individuals, sometimes in our opposition to God, when we recognize our corruption, it brings about petitioning for mercy. However, when all is said and done "our comeliness is still turned into corruption" enwrapped in this poem, and taken from Daniel 10:8. Nothing can change if we are not covered by the blood of Jesus. The overall theme of this poem is to look to God's deliverance and mighty power. It is important to appreciate the fact that, just as how God can make man from the very dust, and breathe into him life, similarly, God can use a poet and breathe life into the words to enhance the understanding of the Book of Daniel. You can consider poetry as another way God is using to inspire, set afire and require us to see His power. The poet then becomes a mouthpiece. Listen and consider the words "in softest blessedness" which exemplifies the pleasing quality of God. The form and structure are simple and easy to follow as a medium for understanding the workings of God and the mental, emotional, and physical frailty of those created in His image. This explicatory poem does not remove itself from the prophecy as history center, as it's taken from the Book of Daniel that runs through all the verses. I challenge you to find more beauty and truth in this poetry.

Chapter 10 Prayer

Lord, please hear my prayer, hear my cry today, save me and deliver. Forgive me and place an edge around me, let your angels surround me. Show yourself mighty to save, show yourself strong to deliver. I reach in confidence to you to your awesome blessedness. In victory let me stand, in Jesus' awesome name. Amen.

Personal Reflections

_____

_____

_____

_____

_____

_____

_____

_____

Daniel 11

"Also I in the first year of Darius the Mede, even I, stood to confirm and to strengthen him. And now will I shew thee the truth. Behold, there shall stand up yet three kings in Persia; and the fourth shall be far richer than they all: and by his strength through his riches he shall stir up all against the realm of Grecia. And a mighty king shall stand up, that shall rule with great dominion, and do according to his will. And when he shall stand up, his kingdom shall be broken, and shall be divided toward the four winds of heaven; and not to his posterity, nor according to his dominion which he ruled: for his kingdom shall be plucked up, even for others beside those. And the king of the south shall be strong, and one of his princes; and he shall be strong above him, and have dominion; his dominion shall be a great dominion. And in the end of years they shall join themselves together; for the king's daughter of the south shall come to the king of the north to make an agreement: but she shall not retain the power of the arm; neither shall he stand, nor his arm: but she shall be given up, and they that brought her, and he that begat her, and he that strengthened her in these times. But out of a branch of her roots shall one stand up in his estate, which shall come with an army, and shall enter into the fortress of the king of the north, and shall deal against them, and shall prevail: And shall also carry captives into Egypt their gods, with their princes, and with their precious vessels of silver and of gold; and he shall continue more years than the king of the north. So the king of the south shall come into his kingdom, and shall return into his own land. But his sons shall be stirred up, and shall assemble a multitude of great forces: and one shall certainly come, and overflow, and pass through: then shall he return, and be stirred up, even to his fortress. And the king of the south shall be moved with choler, and shall come forth and fight with him, even with the king of the north: and he shall set forth a great multitude; but the multitude shall be given into his hand. And when he hath taken away the multitude, his heart shall be lifted up; and he shall cast down many ten thousands: but he shall not be strengthened by it. For the king of the north shall return, and shall set forth a multitude greater than the former, and shall certainly come after certain years with a great army and with much riches. And in those times there shall many stand up against the king of the south: also the robbers of thy people shall exalt themselves to establish the vision; but they shall fall. So the king of the north shall come, and cast up a mount, and take the most fenced cities: and the arms of the south shall not withstand, neither his chosen people, neither shall there be any strength to withstand. But he that cometh against him shall do according to his own will, and none shall stand before him: and he shall stand in the glorious land, which by his hand shall be consumed. He shall also set his face to enter with the strength of his whole kingdom, and upright ones with him; thus shall he do: and he shall give him the daughter of women, corrupting her: but she shall not stand on his side, neither be for him. After this shall he turn his face unto the isles, and shall take many: but a prince for his

187

own behalf shall cause the reproach offered by him to cease; without his own reproach he shall cause it to turn upon him. Then he shall turn his face toward the fort of his own land: but he shall stumble and fall, and not be found. Then shall stand up in his estate a raiser of taxes in the glory of the kingdom: but within few days he shall be destroyed, neither in anger, nor in battle. And in his estate shall stand up a vile person, to whom they shall not give the honour of the kingdom: but he shall come in peaceably, and obtain the kingdom by flatteries. And with the arms of a flood shall they be overflown from before him, and shall be broken; yea, also the prince of the covenant. And after the league made with him he shall work deceitfully: for he shall come up, and shall become strong with a small people. He shall enter peaceably even upon the fattest places of the province; and he shall do that which his fathers have not done, nor his fathers' fathers; he shall scatter among them the prey, and spoil, and riches: yea, and he shall forecast his devices against the strong holds, even for a time. And he shall stir up his power and his courage against the king of the south with a great army; and the king of the south shall be stirred up to battle with a very great and mighty army; but he shall not stand: for they shall forecast devices against him. Yea, they that feed of the portion of his meat shall destroy him, and his army shall overflow: and many shall fall down slain. And both these kings' hearts shall be to do mischief, and they shall speak lies at one table; but it shall not prosper: for yet the end shall be at the time appointed. Then shall he return into his land with great riches; and his heart shall be against the holy covenant; and he shall do exploits, and return to his own land. At the time appointed he shall return, and come toward the south; but it shall not be as the former, or as the latter. For the ships of Chittim shall come against him: therefore he shall be grieved, and return, and have indignation against the holy covenant: so shall he do; he shall even return, and have intelligence with them that forsake the holy covenant. And arms shall stand on his part, and they shall pollute the sanctuary of strength, and shall take away the daily sacrifice, and they shall place the abomination that maketh desolate. And such as do wickedly against the covenant shall he corrupt by flatteries: but the people that do know their God shall be strong, and do exploits. And they that understand among the people shall instruct many: yet they shall fall by the sword, and by flame, by captivity, and by spoil, many days. Now when they shall fall, they shall be holpen with a little help: but many shall cleave to them with flatteries. And some of them of understanding shall fall, to try them, and to purge, and to make them white, even to the time of the end: because it is yet for a time appointed. And the king shall do according to his will; and he shall exalt himself, and magnify himself above every god, and shall speak marvellous things against the God of gods, and shall prosper till the indignation be accomplished: for that that is determined shall be done. Neither shall he regard the God of his fathers, nor the desire of women, nor regard any god: for he shall magnify himself above all. But in his estate shall he honour the God of forces: and a god whom his fathers knew not shall he honour with gold, and silver, and with precious stones, and pleasant things. Thus shall he do in the most strong holds with a strange god, whom he shall acknowledge and increase with glory: and he shall cause them to rule over many, and shall divide the land for gain. And at the time of the end shall the king of the south push at him: and the king of the north shall come against him like a whirlwind, with chariots, and with horsemen, and with many ships; and he shall enter into the countries, and shall overflow and pass over. He shall enter also into the glorious land, and many countries shall be overthrown: but these shall escape out of his hand, even Edom, and Moab, and the chief of the children of Ammon. He shall stretch forth his hand also upon the countries: and the land of Egypt shall not escape. But he shall have power over the treasures of gold and of silver, and over all the precious things of Egypt: and the Libyans and the Ethiopians shall be at his steps. But tidings out of the east and out of the north shall trouble him: therefore he shall go forth with great fury to destroy, and utterly to make away many. And he shall plant the tabernacles of his palace between the seas in the glorious holy mountain; yet he shall come to his end, and none shall help him." (Daniel 11).

For Midnight Comes: Whirlwind, Chariots, Horsemen, & Ships

— **"Then shall the Kingdom of Heaven be likened unto ten virgins ….."**— **Matthew 25:1-13**

So elated that Jesus is the same yesterday, today, and forever
(Hebrews 13:8)
And knowing that Satan is the great deceiver
Creating difficulties of life, thinking he's clever
For God knows about the pain Satan's rebellion has delivered!
Don't blame God for the things that come upon man; it's past time
to understand
God is love: a contrast of the enemy – Satan's grandstand!
The rest of the universe in observation. Whilst Earth is lashed with
Satan's wrath
Christ Jesus died, shed His blood to show us the path
To righteousness and everlasting life – the story of God's loving
heart!
Whilst the fallen angels, on the road of the damned
Marshaling and masquerading, in unholy celebration
With the dragon, beast, and false prophets in a threefold union!
Then Satan shall come as an angel of dazzling light

The fallen angels in an imitation of dead family members to excite
In a false imitation of Christ's mightiness, power, awesome majesty,
and sight!
For Jesus Christ will come, in power and glory,
The language of salvation disclosed, the everlasting love of God for
Man, in this mind-blowing epic revelatory!

In the first year of Darius the Mede (Daniel 6)
Angel Gabriel now confirms, strengthening Darius and the
administration of Babylon in Daniel's time of need
Daniel was in the lion's den for the presidents and princes conspired.
Darius was forced to decree
Miraculously, though, an angel came and closed the lion's mouths; a
miracle indeed!
Truly, we're blessed that Michael is the Archangel, director of
Heaven's breed
For angels are God's messengers at our every need
At God's command, angels fly in urgent speed
Protecting the fallen to meet our every distress
And fight our battles to the uttermost of success!
For here is the truth: the sum of the matter
Three more kings shall stand up in Persia
The fourth king shall be much richer, mightier, and stronger. Then,
he'll stir up all against Greece
Giving a kick to peace!
For after the death of Cyrus the king of Persia
Three more kings arose one after the other
Cambyses (530-522), and another:
the usurper (522), called the False Smerdis – or Bardiya
Darius the first (522-486), here's the sum of the matter
Cyrus the king and Darius the first both issued decrees to rebuild the

temple – must remember
Now, the fourth king (486-465) was Ahasuerus, called Xerxes –
husband of Queen Esther
He spent four years assembling supplies and manpower
For a military expedition against Greece. He was the fourth king,
mightier, stronger, and richer
His army contingents consisted of forty nations
Persians in turbans, Assyrians in brass helmets, Colchians in wooden
hats, Thracians in fox-skin caps, Ethiopians in leopard skins. The
march was on, and many more – on a military declaration
They marched from their homeland
To the battles of Salamis (480), and Plataea (479), in Greece to
complete defeat
Where the metallic silver kingdom and the metallic brass kingdom
in a prophetic competition met! No surrender, no retreat.

Therefore, a mighty king shall stand in great dominion
In exploit and in rule, establishing Greece as a great kingdom
He crossed over the Hellespont into Asia in a historical conquest
Conquering and conquering, this kingdom of the belly and thighs
of brass, moving swiftly never to rest
Death rode upon his favored horse Bucephalus: graceful, young and
strong
Then his kingdom was divided; he never lasted long (Alexander the
Great)
His kingdom then divided. His four generals fought
Cassander claimed the west, and Lysimachus claimed the north
Seleucus claimed the east, and Ptolemy claimed the south
Syria's rulers designated, as the kings of the north
Egypt's rulers designated, as the kings of the south
Jerusalem in between – Syria and Egypt – to the north and south

All the kings of Egypt were called Ptolemy
We are treading on destiny
All the kings of Syria were called Antiochus or Seleucus
Each identified by a number in name, kingdoms of fame, kingdoms
of dust
Antiochus two and Ptolemy two then made an alliance
In a physical compliance
With the daughter of the king of the south
In marriage to the king of the north
For convenience, Antiochus two divorced his first wife Laodice
In order to marry the daughter of Ptolemy, the king of the south,
Berenice
Although Berenice had a son
Still, it could not suffice the relation
Antiochus two put away Berenice and took Laodice back
Laodice, in revenge, killed them all in a precisionary attack
Now the king of the west and king of the east were both consumed
by the king of the north and the king of the south
Therefore, all the kings of the north
And all the kings of the south
In continual feuds
Crisscrossing over many years over Blessed Palestine, land of the
Jews!

The king of the north, on the attack, shall return
With an army greater than the former; the south would mourn
Then, the robbers of God's people
Arose, devouring, breaking and trampling (Daniel 7:7; Daniel 8:13)
In an alliance, Antiochus three, King of the north
Went up against Ptolemy five of Egypt, king of the south
And when the battle was done, Antiochus Epiphanies, king of the

north

With grip firmly on the pleasant lands of Jerusalem and Judah – it was a terrible and tragic fate

Still, this was not the "abomination that makes desolate"

For Jesus indicated that it would appear after his day

A future time of fulfilled prophecy causes Man to tremble and causes Man to pray

It's the "robbers of thy people" in the conquest of "the glorious land" (Daniel 11:14)

In a corrupting of "the daughter of women" (Daniel 11:19-26),

(Julius Caesar and his affair with Queen Cleopatra of Egypt)

Then, another caused the reproach to cease (assassination of Julius Caesar on the Ides on March, 44 BC, with sixty fellow Romans led by Cassius Longinus)

He stumbled and fell never to be. Still no peace (death of Cassius Longinus)

For then came the raiser of taxes in the glory of the kingdom (Augustus Caesar, founder of the Roman Empire), (The Birth of Jesus, Luke 2:1-11)

Emperors called Augustus would come

Then came the "contemptible person" in total control of the kingdom

Entering with peace and flatteries

But after the league made with him shall work deceitfully (Constantine the Great- Daniel 11:23)

This medieval papacy from smallness finally grows into position

The oratory of the Pope: inspired the crusades

Wrestling the Holy Land from the Muslims: rendering safe for Christians and never fades (Islam – Dark Ages- 5 & 6 trumpets of Revelation)

Therefore: the papacy was emboldened by the Middle East crusades
Then initiated the European crusades against the Christian "heretics"
Those sincere believers of God's "holy covenant: in a decimated
arithmetic
Exalted and magnified himself above God
Changed Mount Sinai, Ten Commandments of the Lord
With hired armies achieved political ends
Papacy putting its trust in the "god of fortress" with no pretense
(Daniel 11:38)
And the new god with all her purity and motherly compassion
To be honored with gold, silver, and precious stones: occupied in
Catholic devotion
Isn't she the blessed Virgin: in a prominent place than her Divine
Son
For Jesus is the "prince of the covenant"
This is all about worship and the Ten Commandments: and war on
the remnant
The "abomination that makes desolate," cannot be confined
To the king of the north, Antiochus Epiphanes: nor so defined
It is the practice and belief: that leads people away from the priestly
ministry of Christ
Depriving access to the "prince of the covenant" with deceit against
His sacrifice
The pope exalted himself above God: speaking marvelous things
until the indignation was accomplished
It's not finished: don't be astonished
Verse 3 to verse 4, Medo-Persia
The great metallic silver
Verse 4 to verse 14: Greece
In full brass: to conquer and increase

Verse 14 to verse 22, Rome

Iron movement, a man and the dragon kingdom

Verse 23 to verse 30: military religiopolitical power of the papacy

Verse 31 to verse 36: spiritual conquest of the papacy: and its destiny

Verse 40 to 45: midnight is coming, time of the end (1798 – end of
the 1260 days prophecy – deadly wound to the papacy – French
Revolution Revelation 11, birthplace of atheism)

So, the king of the north is symbolically Babylon and then!

The king of the south is symbolically Egypt: now it's time to
understand

The prophecy is sure: 42 months or 1260 years (Revelation 11:1–4)

Remember a day is still a prophetic year: in this prophetic affair
(Ezekiel 4:6; Num 14:34)

Where the two witnesses did their work in sackcloth: the old and
the New Testaments

Outlawed for 1260 prophetic years: by the kingdom of governments

They laid dead in the streets of the great city: symbolically called
Sodom and Egypt (Revelation 11:8; French Revolution/ birthplace
of atheism/deadly wound to the papacy)

The whole nation denied God, due to the hypocrisy seen of the
papacy: the hypocrite!

Democratic liberalism of the government; some say: Better for all
Wherein Constitutional rights are enthralled

The left and the right as symbols: of the French Revolution

King of the south: now a revolution: for atheism, standing against
the commandments of the true Kingdom!

Like a true King of the north: in much fury
Ready to destroy in all his glory
Counterfeiting the Savior: in a purported rapture
Comes Satan as an unholy deliverer

197

By any means necessary: must ascend on that holy mountain (Isaiah 14:13)

Going up against the ever-living fountain

To claim the prize of the king of the north

Herein the expression rearranged: of the now king of the north and now king of the south

For before Daniel 2: before Nebuchadnezzar entered the pleasant land of Palestine

Prophetically designed!

Egypt then king of the south pushed against Babylon; then king of the north

Babylon then pushed back and entered the promised land

In captivity: Daniel, Shadrach, Meshach, and Abednego: in actions, preached the message of salvation

Babylon would fall to the Medes and Persians

They came from the north and east of Babylon

Whose king was Cyrus: the anointed one: a type of Jesus: also, king of the north

But Nebuchadnezzar meant to rule forever

So, he built an idol in Daniel 3: a statue of gold: trying to be clever!

And all who did not bow down in worship: would be killed

Know now: for midnight comes: When everything will be fulfilled

The symbolic history of Daniel one, two, three, four, five, and six

Reflects the symbolic history of Daniel 11:40–45:now be transfixed!

Who then: is the true king of the north: who will soon arise?

The kings of history: the papacy: the dragon: or Christ?

Midnight: the darkest time of earth's history

Must and shall dispel its mystery!

For Satan shall come as an angel of dazzling light

With fallen angels masquerading as resurrected family members: to excite

The dragon – prince of the air

To capture all in his snare

The beast from the sea

Woe to all: now is the time from sin to flee

The beast from the earth

Satan imitating the king of the north

Dragon: beast: false prophet: in a threefold union

What is there not to understand?

Catholicism: Protestantism: and the

dragon

Satan tabernacle in the glorious mountain

Yet his end shall be final and astounding!

For Michael stands up, in a whirlwind, with chariots, horsemen, and

ships (Isaiah 66:15)

Like a whirlwind, a coming in the air; read the script

And ships – Satan's counterfeit will be eclipsed!

With chariots and horsemen. There is the land

God Almighty in His final command

For the real king of the north

From the beginning of time to the manger of His birth

When on Calvary He died for the sins of earth

Now, coming in clouds of glory, as King of kings

And Lord of lords

Of the heavens and the earth

The great, the mighty, awesome God

Whose protective power and protective blood transcends in His

enduring love!

End.

Reflections

It is quite instructive to hear intellectuals expound in surprise as they discover such rich and thorough history lessons in the Book of Daniel. Many are also surprised to find such amazing exegesis coming out in poetry from the Book of Daniel. I do declare that Daniel is of itself poetry of historic and prophetic dimensions. As you continue to peruse this poetic work, please allow for understanding and knowledge on Daniel and the entire Bible to increase. The word is prophecy, for the Book of Daniel is replete with it. We are given the word so how much more proof do we seek? What is meant by prophecy? It is prediction, declaration of the divine will, and purpose – period. "Pro" equals "forward", and the question is: are we moving forward, are things being fulfilled as prophecy dictates? You can see the truth and appreciation of God in this poetry. As the contravention of deceit and purity continues to haunt these poems, we can see that Satan who might seem to bring light, is a farce. As we look for beauty and artistry, the word "masquerading" comes to mind. One can compose an entire sociological exploration with the connotations of this word. It makes clear of things and people being not what they seem. I am thankful that Jesus Christ is the same yesterday, today, and forever (Hebrews 13:8). The thought of a real superhero, deliver or savior permeates these lines – where mankind is looking for something bigger than themselves. The important words here are man and God. The created and the creator. My challenge to you is to search to find more beauty and truth within these poetic lines, like in your search and exploration of the most popular Broadway shows or latest genre of film and movies.

Chapter 11 Prayer

Dear Loving Father, your awesome mighty power come, descend. I just need you and your protection in this time of the end. Forgive your people and draw all to understand your plan of salvation. For the coming of the Lord is near; this is totally clear. Oh, Almighty God, we are thankful that your appearance is certain. So, deliver us with a mighty hand and save us in your loving embrace. For you are mighty to save! To you, all glory belongs, and majesty, and power. Forever and ever in Jesus' name. Amen.

Personal Reflections

_____

_____

_____

_____

_____

_____

_____

_____

_____

Daniel 12

"And at that time shall Michael stand up, the great prince which standeth for the children of thy people: and there shall be a time of trouble, such as never was since there was a nation even to that same time: and at that time thy people shall be delivered, every one that shall be found written in the book. And many of them that sleep in the dust of the earth shall awake, some to everlasting life, and some to shame and everlasting contempt. And they that be wise shall shine as the brightness of the firmament; and they that turn many to righteousness as the stars for ever and ever. But thou, O Daniel, shut up the words, and seal the book, even to the time of the end: many shall run to and fro, and knowledge shall be increased. Then I Daniel looked, and, behold, there stood other two, the one on this side of the bank of the river, and the other on that side of the bank of the river. And one said to the man clothed in linen, which was upon the waters of the river, How long shall it be to the end of these wonders? And I heard the man clothed in linen, which was upon the waters of the river, when he held up his right hand and his left hand unto heaven, and sware by him that liveth for ever that it shall be for a time, times, and an half; and when he shall have accomplished to scatter the power of the holy people, all these things shall be finished. And I heard, but I understood not: then said I, O my Lord, what shall be the end of these things? And he said, Go thy way, Daniel: for the words are closed up and sealed till the time of the end. Many shall be purified, and made white, and tried; but the wicked shall do wickedly: and none of the wicked shall understand; but the wise shall understand. And from the time that the daily sacrifice shall be taken away, and the abomination that maketh desolate set up, there shall be a thousand two hundred and ninety days. Blessed is he that waiteth, and cometh to the thousand three hundred and five and thirty days. But go thou thy way till the end be: for thou shalt rest, and stand in thy lot at the end of the days." (Daniel 12).

Redeemed! When Michael Shall Descend

— "… I live by faith of the Son of God, who loved me, and gave Himself for me" — Galatians 2:20

Redeemed how I love to proclaim it: Redeemed by the blood of the lamb (Frances J. Crosby)

Lord: I'm fearful: I'm fearful for my life
It has been hard: struggles have been long: difficulties rife amidst the strife
I've been caught in a survival mode: on my back: under attack
The enemy not letting me alone: that's the fact
The whole world in utter turmoil
Leaders in the world: even leaders in the church are untrustworthy: come anoint my head with oil
Spreading the word and the great commission
This should be the mission!
But: it's lacking: Fast track: let us catch the vision
Now petitioning you for a miracle: for not only me in deep trouble
This world is in dire need: for each and every soul: remove the obstacles
Help us lord: let the angels fight our battles

You declared: that the battle is not ours: but the Lord's (2 Chronicles
20:15)
I'm claiming it today from your words
For your word is sure: sharper than any two-edged sword: this is the
word of God
I'm standing at the river Hiddekel: for deliverance
Secure our soul for Christ's intercession: remove obstacles: remove
hindrance.

Throughout my life and throughout my days
In the ups and downs, my disappointments and fears,
There remains only one hope – one God – who cares
Who gave His only begotten Son to die for you and me
In spite of my wrongs, my sins, messed up ways, wrong trajectory
The story of my life, the story of my family
Though God investigates and judges, His blood makes me rise and
sets me free!
For when Christ's intercession is done
Coming to His great and final conclusion
My God will stand up, bringing deliverance and redemption!
The clouds will roll back as a scroll
My God and Savior to extol
The trumpet of the Lord shall sound – His mouth shall carry a sword
Though beleaguered, redeemed from sin, we'll rise and soar
For at the trumpet of the Lord God Almighty
My Savior and king – He will save us; protect and guide me!

This was in the third year of Cyrus, king of Persia, in Daniel ten
When the angel Gabriel started explaining this vision, then,
With Daniel secluded by the river Tigris or Hiddekel
And where Daniel petitioned God for another miracle

Continuing throughout Daniel eleven
Bringing us to the crucible, to the dawn of the Redeemer's coming
in heaven!
In this great and final conclusion
Of the angel Gabriel's summation
For the king of the north rampaged against the saints
Until he met his ruin, as Christ's intercession is done and hearing the
saints' complaints!
Then, there was a time of trouble – such as never was a nation
Michael stands up, bringing deliverance and redemption! (Daniel
12:1)

Even at that time of trouble: which was as never was a nation ever
Then, Michael, the great prince will stand and deliver! (Daniel
7:9-14; Daniel 8:14)
Now, the investigative judgment was done
The sanctuary has been cleansed. Here comes our Savior – the only
begotten Son!
Everyone whose name was written in the book of life
And many who sleep in the dust: shall rise to everlasting life!
In favorable phrase, and respectful comment, I hereby present
"And those who are wise shall shine as the firmament
And those who turn many to righteousness, like the stars forever and
ever" (Daniel 12:3)
So, come all with sin oppressed: mercy's door quiver: accept the
savior!
For Jesus Christ is whom God had sent (John 17:3)
To bear all sins upon the cross: a permanent replacement!
Now triumphant to redeem us!
Sailing on whirlwind clouds, with chariots and horsemen: to gather
all the righteous!

Both those that are alive: and the dead in Christ: first shall rise! (1
Thessalonians 4:16-17)
In full view of the onlooking millions across the universe and skies
The High Priest of the Heavenly Sanctuary reverses the sure death
sentence of the repentant man!
With His crucifixion-wounded hands
Early though the books foretold of tribulations and death
(Revelation 2:10; Matthew 24:9; Revelation 3:10)
But now this glorious rhyme testifies of deliverance, yet! (Daniel
12:1-2; Revelation 20)
Some unrighteous persons, though, are raised from the dead, along
with the resurrected many (Daniel 12:1-2)
Like the high priest who put Him on oath, asking: "Are you the
begotten Son? This isn't funny".
Jesus' answer required your attention:
"Hereafter you will see the Son of Man...coming on the clouds of
Heaven! (Matthew 26:64)
For as Jesus traveled on clouds to the judgment at the end of the
2300 year-days, (Daniel 7:13; Daniel 8:14)
Saints of God – get ready for the getting up praise: a time of praise,
of praise! and more praise!
Jesus will arise – and, similarly, on clouds of glory. His triumphant
travel to earth
For all those who pierced Him must be convinced of His story and
His worth! (Revelation 1:7)

Daniel then was told: Shut up the words – seal the Book until the
end
The message must be preached; all must understand then
For Gabriel promised: the wise shall shine like the stars (Daniel 12:3)
All the worlds must know of His unconditional love, including

earth, all planets, even Mars

Remember the head of gold as Babylon? The ram as Medio-Persia?

The goat as Greece? Daniel's day empires

So, the events to be shut up are at the time of the end

For the man "clothed in linen", at the beginning of the vision

This is Michael our prince, hovering over the river Tigris or
Hiddekel (Daniel 10:21; Daniel 12:1)

Flanked by an angel honor guard, totally visible,

Was questioned by Daniel. "Lord! how long? what shall the issues of
these things?"

For it shall be for a time, two times, and half a time. Earth in pain;
Earth will ring!

The Lord declined to answer his second question: ordering Daniel
to go

When the Son of Man swore by the Living God, the message
followed (Daniel 12:7; Revelation 10)

At the time of the end of the 1260 years (Daniel 7:25)

Wonderful light would dawn on the message of 1260 days

Knowledge shall increase – increased understanding of Bible
prophecy (Daniel 12:3)

He did not provide events for the close of the 1290 days, nor for the
beginning or end of the 1335 days

Though blessedness shall attend the persons who wait to the end of
1335 days

But Daniel shall rest and stand in his allotted place!

Though spending the intervening years in the grave

When Michael shall descend. Then, and only then, Daniel will stand
with the saved!

For most of all, God is love

And His love through His begotten Son shines to all from up above

His promise is sure to all who live for God

At this momentous end of the age

The promise comes to let you know: God is love; God cares!

End.

Reflections

This is the final summation of the deliverance and redemption that is in store for all the redeemed of earth. I'm certainly privileged to be chosen as this poetic conduit in bringing into context the awe-inspiring Book of Daniel through poetry. I wonder why God chose a sinner like me, to tell about this wonder-working, miracle-working, awesome power of God in poetic formation, of this amazing story in poetry? And my answer is: to show His saving grace, love, and mighty power. It is now time to proclaim this amazing love story to the streets of every village, town, city, and country. The tale has been told, now prophesy! This is a personal account of God leading in the life of Daniel, of you and me. It is all up to you now. Be brave – step out in faith. You can continue to appreciate the revelatory poetical beauty in this poetry, by looking at the action and resolution of the poems; rooted in the Book of Daniel but with supporting evidence from the other Books. The tale is a compelling one of steadfastness, failure through ignorance, and an inability to recognize the message of salvation. The word redemption stares back at us – we can feel it already as we choose and acknowledge the power of God. In its words of promise for those who choose, this poem, and all the poems in this book of 'The Language of Daniel", reiterates the glory of the risen Christ, who came in human form for accessibility, to bring accountability – who was rejected most piteously but who because of who HE IS has remained with HAND OUTSTRETCHED TO SAVE. I challenge you today to find more beauty in Christ through this poetry.

Chapter 12 Prayer

My God, my God, my God, do not forsake us. Thank you for your plan of salvation. Thank you for your redemptive power. Thank you for your forgiveness and love even before we ask – because it's freely given. Thank you for hearing and for answering my prayer. What a mighty and great God we serve! Thank you most of all for your love that is demonstrated in your gifting of your only begotten Son. Thank you for using this poetic format in saving your people graciously. Thank you, for the time is at hand when your people will be delivered and taken home to live with you throughout eternity. This is my prayer of thanksgiving in Jesus' name. Amen.

Personal Reflections

_____

_____

_____

_____

_____

_____

_____

_____

_____

About the Author

Poet, a preacher of the word, community liaison, community activist, servant of the living God, James C. Richmond is a prolific, evocative spoken-word artist who – through his poetry – enlarges our comprehension of the world around us and helps us to grasp our life's journey. He champions community empowerment in everything he puts his heart into and sets his mind on, promoting and propagating culture and urging all to embrace their religious destiny. Through his endeavors and poetry, Richmond encourages us to tap into our rich cultural identities, both individually and collectively, to develop a better understanding and appreciation of each other. He is a consummate performer of his poetry with a career that spans over 30 years. He has been a featured writer in several community newspapers and magazines in the United States and the Caribbean over the years, contributing articles and poetry to a variety of publications. Richmond has self-published three other books of poetry: namely, "On the Window of My Skin" (2006), "Where the Pomeroon Meets" (1997), and "Reflections of Today" (1990). He has also written poetry on the books of both Daniel and Revelation from the Bible. Richmond is a Christian and he loves the Lord. Stay tuned. Be blessed!

Epilogue

King Nebuchadnezzar was only in his second year of reign, but obviously well learned, astute, powerful, and brutal (Daniel 2:1), when he had his first dream. He was troubled by the dream and sought out his most intelligent doctors in magic, astrology, sorcery, and the powerful Chaldeans, to help him to remember. However, none of them could, or even conspire a dream. They could not fool him. This most powerful of kings decreed that all the wise men should be put to death because they could not remind him of the dream nor give the true meaning of the dream (Daniel 2:13). Despite being such a powerful king, he could only demonstrate power through, violence, destruction, and death decrees. However, there is a true King of Kings and Lord of Lords, whose love for mankind is supreme, and He is the true director of human affairs; "He sits high and looks low" and His actions are always grounded in love.

This brings me to my favorite verse, which can be found in what can be described as, the most proactive and courageous actionable text of Daniel 2, nestled in verse 16, where Daniel literally demonstrated pure faith in God. It states, "Then Daniel went in, and desired of the king that he would give him time and that he would shew the king the interpretation" (Daniel 2:16). Although the wise men saw impossibility, Daniel saw possibility. When they saw their fallibility, Daniel saw his capability. He displayed two great character traits of those who trust entirely in God's help. First, Daniel demonstrated courage in venturing into the presence of the King and, secondly, humility in asking the King to give him time to consult with his friends and the awesome power of God through prayer. Instead of those who relied on their own wisdom, he relied on God.

It is said that "prayer is power" – but many of us don't have the courage to believe that our prayers will be answered. Many times, in my life, when faced with troubling decrees, and daunting situations, and it seems like the door of death is slamming in my face, my faith has given way to fear. Despite my prayers, in the urgency of the situation, my courage has been lost. But knowing that God is able, I just leave it at the Throne of Grace for the answer – be it a yes or a no or wait. It is said that, to be successful in a relationship, you must first have trust. It's obvious that Daniel trusted God because he had a relationship with Him. Are you in a relationship with God? Do you really trust God? Do you trust Him so much that you feast on His every word? Do you really want to know why I hold this verse of Daniel 2 verse 16 as a favorite? It builds my faith, knowing that, in trusting God – with whom I already have a relationship – everything's going to be all right in the end. Just "give me some time, my Nebuchadnezzar", and I'll show you! In the Book of James 5:16, it is states: "The effectual fervent prayer of a righteous man availeth much". As we come to the close, John 5:14 asserts "And this is the confidence that we have in Him, that, if we ask anything according to His will, He hears us". As the songwriter says, "Only trust Him; Only trust Him; Only trust him now. He will save you; He will save you; He will save you now." May our loving lord save us all. This is my fervent prayer for me and for you.

Endorsements

"The Book of Daniel with its complexity and prophetic themes offers an opportunity for poetic utterances. The author of this book, "The Language of Daniel", James Richmond, has done an outstanding job in presenting in creative language such deep and prophetic truths. May the readers of this book be inspired as a result of reading and digesting these imaginative thoughts". – Dr, G. Earl Knight, President of Atlantic Union Conference of SDA

"James Richmond has taken his writing skills to another level. By blending theological insight and poetic talent, he has produced a literary gem on Bible prophecy. This exposé on the Book of Daniel allows the reader to experience the prophet's emotional journey on a personal level. Ultimately the book enhances one's understanding of the prophet and his prophesies". – Dr. Daniel Honore, President of Northeastern Conference of SDA

"James Richmond has used his keen interest in poetry to comment on the Book of Daniel in a way that is easily understood. This book is a useful resource for all who are interested in Daniel's writings". – Lois King Ph.D., CFLE

"This amazing book, "The Language of Daniel" – based on the

220

biblical Book of Daniel – is highly recommended reading. It is a great way of getting acquainted with the word of God for first-timers and lovers of poetry and prophesy. This book creates pictures on the mind and is timely, and applicable, for our times". – Bianel Lara, Ph.D. candidate, Publishing Director, GNYC

"James Richmond brings a fresh approach to appreciating one of the most interesting books of the Bible – the Book of Daniel. His unique poetic style brings the stories and prophecies of this magnificent book to life in a way that will inspire you to mine its pages for deeper truths". – Eric Flickinger, pastor and presenter, It Is Written

"In 'The Language of Daniel', Richmond uses his artistic writing style to carry one into a picturesque realm where the union of prophecy and poetry is celebrated. He successfully guides the reader to embrace prophetic truths and juxtaposes them with poetic themes. A great read for all!" – Dr. David McKenzie, Director SDA Youth Ministry, Atlantic Union Conference of SDA

Works Consulted

Compiled by Patrick Etoughé Anani, PhD

Boadt, Lawrence, éd. *The Hebrew prophets: visionaries of the ancient world.* 1st ed.

> The Lion classic Bible series. Oxford, England: Lion Publishing, 1998.

Doukhan, Jacques. Daniel 11 decoded: an exegetical, historical, and theological study.

> Berrien Springs, MI: Andrews University Press, 2019.

_____ *Daniel: the vision of the end.*

> Berrien Springs, MI: Andrews University Press, 1987.

_____ *Secrets of Daniel: wisdom and dreams of a Jewish prince in exile.*

> Hagerstown, MD: Review and Herald Pub. Association, 2000.

Maxwell, C. Mervyn, John Steel, et James Converse. *God Cares. Vol. 1,*

Nampa, Idaho; Oshawa, Ont.: Pacific Press Pub. Association, 1981.

Pfandl, Gerhard. *Daniel: the seer of Babylon.*

Hagerstown, Md: Review and Herald Pub. Association, 2004.

Shea, William H. *Daniel: a reader's guide.*

Nampa, Idaho: Pacific Press Pub. Association, 2005.

The Holy Bible, English Standard Version (ESV)

(Wheaton, IL: Crossway Bibles, 2007), BibleWorks, v.9.

The King James study Bible.

Full-Color edition. Nashville, TN: Thomas Nelson Publishers, 2017.

Youngblood, Ronald F., F. F. Bruce, R. K. Harrison, et Thomas Nelson Publishers, éd. *Nelson's illustrated Bible dictionary. New and Enhanced edition.*

Nashville: Thomas Nelson, 2014.

Made in the USA
Middletown, DE
23 April 2022